ADVANCES IN
LIBRARY ADMINISTRATION
AND ORGANIZATION

Volume 1 ● 1982

ADVANCES IN LIBRARY ADMINISTRATION AND ORGANIZATION

Editors: GERARD B. MCCABE
Director of University Libraries
Virginia Commonwealth University

BERNARD KREISSMAN
University Librarian
University of California, Davis

W. CARL JACKSON
University Libraries
Indiana University

VOLUME 1 ● 1982

 JAI PRESS INC.

Greenwich, Connecticut   *London, England*

DEDICATION

Warren N. Boes
1929–1980

The untimely death of Warren N. Boes leaves a void not only for his family, but also for those who worked with him. Warren was an innovator in a profession that sorely lacks innovation, a person full of fresh ideas based on sound judgment from years of experience in the library field. He personified the epitome of the gentleman scholar with the keen sense and reality of a businessman. His devotion to the library field, his keen awareness of future trends, his interest in the training and success of young people as well as his peers both in and out of the profession, and his willingness to give of himself will be sorely missed and remembered by all who knew him.

Without his initial inspiration and encouragement, *Advances in Library Administration and Organization* would not have become a reality. On behalf of JAI Press and the editors, I hereby dedicate this series to my friend, advisor and colleague, Warren N. Boes.

Herbert M. Johnson
Publisher

CONTENTS

IN MEMORIAM

W. Carl Jackson
1923–1981

We sadly acknowledge and express our sympathy at the untimely passing of W. Carl Jackson. Carl's contributions to the field of Library Science are well recognized, and the Press is grateful for his valuable advice and guidance in the formation of *Advances in Library Administration and Organization*.

Herbert M. Johnson
Publisher

INTRODUCTION

The first volume of *Library Literature*, covering the twelve-year period from 1921–1932, included 430 pages and contained an estimated 28,523 entries*, or an average of 2,376 items per year. The most recent available bound volume of that index covers the single year 1979, has 673 pages and contains an estimated 41,800 entries.* Obviously, the volume of published literature about librarianship has grown tremendously, and the trend appears likely to continue.

"Why, then, another library publication?" you might well ask. The justification is not hard to find. According to the sociologists, it is quite customary that, as a profession matures, it becomes increasingly complex and begins to develop areas of specialization, and its published literature keeps pace. Thus, the increase of publishing in the library field is simply a reflection of the growth and increasing maturity of the library profession.

While such growth has occurred steadily since 1876, the last two decades have brought not only significant growth, but more importantly, quantum increases in the complexities of the profession, with the result that the field is quite unlike that as practiced in the 1950s.

It is not technology alone which has sparked the changes, although technology has certainly contributed its share toward changing the outlook of librarians, in changing the policies and operations of libraries, in forcing changes in their budgets, and in breaking down their insularity into what is now a commonly accepted interdependence.

But libraries are also a part of the societies they serve and in which they exist, and changes to or in those societies are inevitably reflected within the libraries. Thus, after the euphoria of the ebullient sixties, most libraries had to make severe adjustments to meet the restraints of the stringent seventies. Now we face what some would call the fearsome eighties, as the nation changes its mood and priorities. While few would argue that the nation's galloping inflation, widely ascribed to uncontrolled federal government spending, needs to be checked and brought under control, librarians are legitimately concerned for the effect on their programs and operations as a result of federal and state tax cuts, budget reductions, and the elimination of long established funding sources.

In developing strategies for accommodating reduced budgets, other factors will need to be considered, not least of which is the rapid erosion of the standard of living for most librarians, as a consequence of the failure of appropriating bodies to allocate salary increases commensurate with the rise in the cost of living. Too many years of fall-short annual salary increases has, in-turn, resulted in a change in the attitude of many librarians and brought a noticeable air of militancy and an increasing tolerance for the process of collective bargaining.

Collective bargaining has also begun to impinge on our so-called professional associations as a result of increasing calls for them to become engaged in this activity. While the issue has as yet hardly become a universal topic, there seems as well to be increasing awareness that librarianship does not in fact have a truly professional association, or any other agency which is concerned with the welfare and status of individual librarians. As far as that goes, there is little agreement as to whether the profession needs a union for collective bargaining or a strong, protective and fully professional association. But, as awareness of this issue widens to a larger, more significant segment of the librarian population, it is likely that major changes in the nature and goals of the American Library Association and/or its subunits, such as the Association of College and Research Libraries and others, will be required. It seems unlikely that these principal organizations of our profession will be allowed to continue their myopic focus on *libraries* and *librarianship* to the exclusion of concern for the economic welfare, status, and work environment of individual *librarians*, particularly as more and more members demand changes.

That same change of attitude of librarians is likely as well to have an impact on the management of libraries. In response to pressure in the 1960s many academic libraries adopted a "collegial" approach to governance, although some have argued that this was largely a facade since the administrative hierarchy remained in place and the collegiality consisted simply of an overlay of committees. The variety of opinions on that issue are no less in the matter of unions in libraries. Some libraries have now had several years of experience with collective bargaining, although the overall percentage of such libraries is quite small. Will the future bring, as some have claimed, unions and collective bargaining to public libraries and faculty status and increased collegiality to academic libraries? It seems unlikely that the latter necessarily precludes collective bargaining and it is equally unlikely that a specific pattern will emerge, but changes are sure to come, and it is almost inevitable that they will result in added complexities for some already beleaguered library administrators.

Regardless of governance, library operational problems will certainly continue to compound. The budget will be a primary concern whether it simply fails to keep pace with rising costs or is actually reduced. The result, reduction of services or operations, will only vary in degree. Such situations usually result in low morale and political turmoil both within and outside the library, as is now evident around the country as public school systems try to close schools in an attempt to stay within their shrinking budgets.

Other challenges include the increasing amount of sophistication of technology, particularly automation, in libraries, along with networking with its attendant complexities and interdependence. For many university libraries, that issue is already sufficiently complex, as they try to weigh their obligations to their state networks, which are connected to one national utility, against perceived benefits from belonging to a different utility which focuses on service to their particular kind of library. For some other university libraries, there is the even more befuddling factor of a regional network perched uneasily between the state network and the national utility.

The issue of professionalism is another urgent matter, within our libraries as well as in our professional associations. With library budgets under ever more pressure, there will be many temptations to use nonprofessional staff for more and more assignments. Thus, it will be necessary for us to more closely analyze our tasks and responsibilities in order to sharpen the definition of just what is professional.

Reduced operating budgets are usually accompanied by reduced capital construction funding. Perforce, many libraries already bursting at the seams will be forced to continue to endure these dificult conditions. Does the solution to overcrowding in the stacks lie in storage buildings or in greater utilization of microfilms? What are the wave effects, such as added staff and operating costs on the one hand and patron resistance and dissatisfaction on the other, of either course.

Collection development will be a matter of increasing concern as our library budgets continue to fail to match strides with the increasing costs of publications. The necessity for honing, ever sharper, our selection skills and our collection development policies will become increasingly essential.

Those collections already in our libraries cannot much longer be ignored. Especially in research libraries, the failure to initiate effective preservation policies and programs can perhaps be compared to living with a time bomb. Although most libraries are, and have long been, aware of their problem, other pressures on the budget usually judged to be more immediate have prevented most libraries from meeting this growing challenge. But, the problem will not go away and can only get worse if it continues to be ignored.

These, and other challenges to the effective operation of our libraries, will be addressed in this and future volumes in this series. Realizing that change begets change, we hope and intend that *Advance in Library Administration and Organization* will be a source of help in anticipating and adapting to these changes that face the profession, to the ultimate benefit of librarians as well as libraries and the publics they serve.

W. Carl Jackson
Indiana University

*Based on a random sample count.

CONTINUITY OR DISCONTINUITY— A PERSISTENT PERSONNEL ISSUE IN ACADEMIC LIBRARIANSHIP

Allen B. Veaner

ABSTRACT

The author traces two decades of rapid change in the character of librarianship and consequent redistribution of duties and responsibilities among various levels of professional and support staff. He contends that the profession of librarianship is characterized by discontinuity rather than the continuity of trades and crafts; that librarians should be concerned with programmatic and decision-making matters supportive of academic programs with technical support in the production area coming from library technicians and assistants. He maintains that new technological developments constantly drive complex duties downward in the work hierarchy while developing new complexities in the programmatic and decision making areas challenge professionals with new responsibilities as they shed duties formerly considered professional. He contends that unlike classified positions, librarianship is not and cannot be a specific aggregate of enumerated duties and responsibilities; rather librarianship is a gestalt, a complex of flexible, interacting functions, ever-changing and ever-adapting, responsive to continuing developments in the fields of library and information science.

Advances in Library Administration and Organization, volume 1, pages 1–20

INTRODUCTION

Academic libraries have become large, complex organizations demanding a broad range of staff to carry out their primary mission of supporting instruction, research and community service. New tools—such as computerized bibliographic networks and commercial data base services—new cataloging codes, new media, the rising expectations of their clientele, and the spread of collective bargaining combine to make the library one of the most complex and rapidly changing units on the modern campus. Positions within the library range in complexity from the simplest production work—such as the clerical task of property stamping a book—to the most sophisticated intellectual work—such as providing advanced reference and research assistance to graduate students, researchers and faculty. Thus it is not surprising that the proper utilization of different categories of staff has come to be an ever more pervasive and difficult problem in academic libraries.

Abstractly stated, the problem of personnel utilization can be postulated as a fundamental question of librarianship: Is the library profession characterized by *discontinuity or continuity*? The answer may have profound implications for the status of librarians, for graduate education in library science, for the academic institution's budget, for collective bargaining, and potentially for class action litigation in the area of equal pay for equal work.[1] Discussions with library directors from member institutions of the Association of Research Libraries suggests that the discontinuity/continuity question is not uncommon but rather varies by degree from one institution to another.[2]

The *discontinuity* model implies that there is a body of constantly advancing professional knowledge, graduate programs of education to impart that knowledge, a category of academic appointees—librarians—dedicated to applying that knowledge in a research university environment, and a category of nonacademic staff to perform designated support functions. The *continuity* model implies that librarianship is more of a craft than profession, that on-the-job learning is completely sufficient, that there is a continuum of knowledge and expertise ranging over all categories of employees, that experience, education or intellectual capacities outside of librarianship equal or surpass graduate professional education in importance and usefulness, and that work in the library forms a continuum characterized by opportunity for indefinite job expansion, unlimited upward mobility, and ever more personal growth.

Historical Development

The growth of North American libraries over the past fifteen to twenty years has gone through two clearly discernible phases which illustrate the two hypothesized models in bold relief.[3] Phase I, the early 1960s, is characterized by an explosive growth of publication, library facilities, and library staff to accommodate rapidly expanding enrollments. A severe shortage of library professionals qualified to cope with expansion leads to a commonplace solution: to get the work done, it is assigned to nonlibrarians available from a pool of highly educated student spouses, faculty spouses, or others, disregarding whether such employees have acquired graduate professional education in librarianship. At the same time, the library profession attempts to slough off "nonprofessional" or clerical duties to appropriate levels of staff while failing to agree on definitions of what is professional and what is not. Further compounding the problem is a failure to administer the differences even when known and articulated.

Phase II comes a decade later when the scenario changes to one of rapid and severe contraction of the educational establishment; the era of continuous growth ends. But the failure of the library profession and the failure of library administrators to come to grips with the duality of professional and support work has already done its damage: there is a perception that two categories of employees are performing widely overlapping functions, seemingly at the same level, but in different employee series with different pay scales and different prerequisites. Other significant consequences include allegations of inequities in classification, charges of failure to provide equal pay for "equal" work, jealousies between librarians and library assistants, misperceptions of who can or should do what. Highly educated employees in support staff roles feel dead-ended, embittered and frustrated, their talents and abilities far surpassing the challenge of their job assignments. In some cases employees on their own seek out more challenging work in the library, distorting existing job classification systems.

Sources of Current Conflicting Concepts in Role Differentiation

Every enterprise is characterized by a wide spectrum of functions and duties in the employment sector, and most seem to boil down to hierarchical models where there are a few persons in administration, an intermediate number of middle management positions, and a great many others in operations and production. This hierarchical model seems especially characteristic of large libraries, perhaps because there is such a vast amount of real production work to do. We must face the fact that libraries, even though they deal with intellectual products and services, are not so unique and distinctive that they differ radically from other service enterprises characterized by high volumes of production work, say a dry cleaning establishment, a garage, or a hospital. Structurally there will be many more similarities than differences in jobs and work requirements. To be sure, the skills required will differ vastly and so will the stock-in-trade, the equipment, the goals and objectives. But there will be striking similarities in structure and function, especially in the distribution of employees as matched to the work to be done. Until the bedpan has been invented that cleans itself, hospital orderlies will be needed; until the maintenance-free fuel system is devised, garages will need to hire carburetor specialists; until the self-shelving book is developed, student aides and library pages will be needed. So will terminal operators, searchers, persons to repair library materials, messengers, copy machine operators, and so forth.[4]

Given the extreme span of activity in the academic library, it is not difficult to identify the wide variety of work to be done and to associate it with the appropriate level of classification and pay. This is an established realm of personnel work and there are experts in position description, classification and pay.[5] As long as libraries deal with vast numbers of diverse physical objects which must be acquired, maintained, processed, or otherwise serviced via high volume transaction systems, they will remain labor-intensive places where most of the work will tend to fall along that part of the spectrum usually designated production work. In circulation, coding, input, shelf maintenance, acquisitions, accounting, and similar activities there will be very large amounts of repetitive production work. There will be lesser quantities of nonrepetitive work involving the creative intellect, for example, original cataloging, reference and research assistance, as well as teaching, but this will nevertheless be production work.[6] There will be major amounts of nonquantifiable, nonproduction work associated with planning, resource allocation, and decision making, that is, administration and management. But as Bayless suggests, to suppose that the various categories of library work can all be done independently of experience, education and ability is to postulate that librarianship is not a profession and that anyone can do any job.[7] This is patently not true of any profession and certainly is not true of librarianship. (It may be that when we use terms like "professional" and "nonprofessional" in the library we confound the issue. While there are experts in every facet of employment—plumbing, law, haircutting, surgery—it is a misuse of nomenclature to suggest that mere facility in a craft is equivalent to the knowledge and expertise gained through graduate professional education and tested by criteria. In universities, it may be better to apply the terms "academic" or "supportive" in place of "professional.")

It is more than half a century since C. C. Williamson in his report on education for librarianship stated that a first prerequisite was to divide the workload into a professional and a support component.[8] Yet many responsibilities which were once professional are no longer so, for the professional decisions have long since been made by a national or regional agency and one can now simply follow the rules. This is where a great deal of trouble lies: some librarians cling to the qualifications by which they were designated professional in the past; they do not recognize that changing times have drained away the professional challenge that once inhered in certain tasks. The result is that nonprofessionals see themselves as doing what "professionals" have always done, and thus see no difference between the two categories. In these instances professional librarianship continues to be measured by the least professional aspects of the work rather than by the most. And some librarians themselves have complicated the problem of upgrading the profession: by clinging to the old indicators and continuing to call them professional, they seem to support the nonprofessionals' claims that they are doing exactly what the designated professionals are doing, and doing it just as well.

In an important and well-written paper, Dougherty has outstandingly limned the role confusion between professionals and other staff. He rightly excoriates the profession for its failure to develop and maintain a clear definition of librarianship and traces to this lack the "growing rift in the relations between professionals and other library staff." It is illuminating to quote this paper *in extenso*:

> Library assistants have become increasingly dissatisfied with their status. Their complaints can be attributed to several factors. Librarians, preoccupied with the desire to improve their own lot, have shown little concern over either the economic welfare or the workplace role of the library assistant.
>
> Librarians, in an effort to improve the utilization of staff, assign tasks identified as unprofessional to their subordinates. Librarians spend more time away from their "desks." They actively engage in the governance of libraries, and they spend more time at conferences. The tasks they performed must now be performed in their absence by assistants. Although this process of reassignment has created new opportunities for library assistants, the added responsibilities too often have not been accompanied by commensurate rewards. There is growing evidence that library assistants perceive that the gap in salaries and other fringe benefits has widened between librarians and themselves rather than narrowed.[9]

If accompanying these attitudes there prevail nonprogrammatic, task-oriented definitions of librarianship along with highly specific delineations of support tasks, including some programmatic responsibilities, it is not unexpected that support staff should be asking questions such as:

1. What is the "real" difference between an "academic" librarian and a nonlibrarian who is employed in a classified job?
2. Why are nonacademic staff unable to advance to the highest grade of their employment series in the same manner as librarians and faculty advance through their academic ranks?
3. What is the relationship between the *qualifications* of a nonacademic employee and that person's current classification and advancement potential?
4. Are there "battlefield commissions," that is, promotions from

nonacademic to academic appointments attributable either to excellent service or high qualifications?

5. How do library assistants acquire their duties and responsibilities? (In principle it is generally agreed that library administrators, usually department heads, assign the duties and responsibilities of assistants and that work is not freely taken on by employees. But in practice the latter has been known to occur.)

In responding to these questions the library administration customarily makes the following points among others:

1. The library director is charged by the institution's president or chancellor or by the personnel department to administer at least two major employment series, a professional series for librarians and a nonprofessional or support series for those employed in non-librarian positions.

2. The library director is not permitted to change the institution's established employment structure.

3. Even if they are not actual faculty appointees, librarians tend to be ranked in parallel with faculty, whereas the nonacademic staff is classified, with job level driven by assigned duties and responsibilities which essentially control the level of classification.

4. Librarians are almost always exempt employees and library assistants (with few exceptions) are nonexempt.

5. A dual employee series implies nothing about the value of human beings in either category. It is not a judgment. It merely signifies that there are different categories of employees for different levels of work. There is a "fence" between the two categories of library jobs and in some library systems there is yet another fence between librarianship and the professoriate.

A philosophical definition of librarianship, one that is not solely or even chiefly task oriented, could contribute to answering the vexing and recurring question: "What is the 'real' difference between nonlibrarians and librarians?" One major, obvious distinction is that it is the academics who carry the library's *programmatic responsibilities*. Employing professional judgment, many categories of librarians make or contribute to the intellectual choices which result in certain resource allocation decisions, decisions which form and drive the library programs supportive of institutional goals, objectives and academic programs. This aspect of responsibility and function is well articulated by that part of the American Library Association's 1972 *Standards for Accreditation* which deals with the curricula of graduate education programs in library science. In characterizing the library profession and the kind of graduate education it requires, the *Standards*, paraphrasing ALA's 1970 policy statement, *Library Education and Personnel Utilization* (LEPU), state:

> Professional responsibilities require special background and education by which the librarian is prepared to identify needs, set goals, analyze problems, and formulate original and creative solutions for them; and to participate in planning, organizing, communicating, and administering programs of services for users of the library's materials and services.[10]

For librarians to fulfill their assignments involving planning, analysis, design, problem solving, and administration, it is essential to have a corps of stable, competent and dedicated classified personnel to carry out the production work—the innumerable tasks and procedures which will flow from the librarians' programmatic decisions. A significant amount of this task-and procedure-oriented work revolves about high production, transaction-oriented systems and will be comparatively routine in nature. A smaller subset of tasks, ascending in challenge and complexity, but still of a production nature, will be reserved for the higher ranks of classified personnel. This is the level commonly designated as paraprofessional. Once it is understood that librarians are concerned chiefly with programmatic matters, with instruction, reference, and research assistance, administration and management, and that support staff employees are mainly concerned with production tasks of varying complexity, the conflicts surrounding role differentiation can at least be explained if not resolved. However, even librarians cannot be entirely free from "production" work as has already been alluded to above and will be further emhasized below.

How the "Peculiarities" of the Library as an Academic Unit Contribute to the Problem

What makes the academic library an especially fertile ground for failure in role differentiation? Actually, a library is a "peculiar" organization on campus. In other academic departments there is an evident and clear distinction between instruction, research, and support. There is general agreement that a lecturer is not the same as a professor, that an administrative asistant, no matter how competent in "running" the department, does not control academic affairs. The least well-defined distinction may be between teaching faculty and teaching assistants (TAs), for both are involved in instruction and research. However, the TA is clearly an apprenticeship which endures only until the candidate gains the doctorate, gets a faculty appointment or drops out of a program. No one TA is a permanent employee as TA.

How different is the library! The library may typically be the largest academic unit on campus and have the largest mix of academic and non-academic staff. Except for student employees—most of whom are assigned routine duties—every incumbent is normally a career employee.

The transience of the student population and the comparatively small number of TAs in each academic department alleviate to some extent the overlaps and ambiguities between faculty and TAs. But not only is the nonacademic staff in the library *not* transient, it also greatly outnumbers the academic staff. But unlike the teaching departments, rare is the library which has sufficiently and properly distinguished the work of academic and nonacademic staff. Several factors can be identified as contributing to the continuing confusion in role differentiation in the academic library:

1. An historical trend of not recognizing or applying appropriate distinctions between academic and nonacademic staff.
2. Insufficiently or inaccurately articulated statements descriptive of librarianship and its character.
3. Popular stereotypes of the librarian as one who "checks out books" or performs generally clerical functions.[11]
4. Continuing assignment to nonacademic staff of responsibility for programmatic decisions.
5. Application of excessively task-oriented, nonconceptual definitions of librarianship and use of inappropriate, industry-derived technical terminology (e.g., "job description") to detail professional positions.
6. A failure to recognize how swiftly the character of librarianship has changed as automation, networking and other influences have swept away complex functions once regarded as the domain of the professional.[12]
7. Inadequate knowledge of library management perhaps attributable in part to the greater emphasis in library school curricula given to technical and historical matters as opposed to the skills required for practical administration.

What Are the Options?

Since these factors have contributed to some instances of persons in different employment series performing similar work, what options exist to rectify the situation? The options suggested below are identified in general philosophical terms rather than being specific to any university. These are but a few of many possibilities; further study and discussion might yield other options.

A. Actions/Options Based on the Discontinuity Model

1. Define clearly and distinctly the duties and responsibilities of library assistants and librarians and explain how each category of employee acquires its duties and responsibilities. Identify classified staff who have been performing essentially programmatic responsibilities or other academic assignments and require them to back off from these assignments; similarly, remove from librarians any nonacademic work they may be doing and reassign to classified staff.

2. Another option based on the discontinuity model is a variation of the above: identify classified staff who have been doing the work of academic appointees and appoint them as librarians subject to the same expectations, and evaluation criteria as the latter, for example, requirements for research, publication, professional participation and community service would apply. If this alternative is unacceptable to employee, return to first alternative above.

B. Option Based on Continuity Model

Declare that librarianship is an art, trade, craft or vocation rather than a profession. Implement an apprenticeship system: all skills to be learned on the job and imparted by training and oral instruction. Library to be managed by a professional administrator and perhaps half a dozen professional deputies or coordinators who may or may not be librarians. Combine library assistants and remaining librarian positions into a new category of employee, perhaps "information processing staff," with a range of salary steps, the whole to be organized according to a variety of functional subdivisions, such as:

Collection development and selection of library materials
Technical processing work
Informational and locational service to the public
Reference and research assistance to the public
Branch library administration
Computerized information retrieval services
Automated library housekeeping services
Collection maintenance and preservation work

C. Option Based on Redefinition of Librarianship

The 1970 LEPU statement specifically affirms that "the library profession has responsibility for defining the training and education required for the preparation of personnel who work in libraries at any level, supportive or professional."[13] This principle is endorsed by the National Librarians Association.[14] Since the profession is responsible for defining its own character and given that librarianship of the 1980's is not that of the fifties or sixties, is it not appropriate and timely that we reconsider the character of our own profession? A third option is available, one that can redefine the functions of the academic and the nonacademic to minimize or remove the ambiguities and overlapping that have beset us. This third option redefines librarianship explicitly in terms designed to establish and maintain discontinuity and allows categorical rejection of Option B.

Discussion

With this background and these proposed options we are now ready for further discussion of the two models postulated at the beginning of this paper. We contend that three series commonly prevailing in academic institutions—librarians, library assistants, and faculty—are discontinuous; they do not merge one into the other. There is no continuum; the duties and responsibilities, methods of appointment, evaluation procedures, career development paths, pay and perquisites—all differ substantially. We claim there is a "fence" between the three series. It is possible to talk, see, and hear through the fence but one cannot cross it except through a special mechanism—the apparatus of open recruitment. This "fence" is an integral part of the structure of the university in Western society and follows an hierarchical model. It is based not on an egalitarian concept but rather on a tradition and a reality, namely that knowledge is possessed by the faculty who agree to teach it to the students and that their joint interaction can create new knowledge. There is no question that this structure is of an elitist character, inasmuch as the university is an elitist institution. Thus the university itself partakes of the character of discontinuity. In the same vein, we claim that librarianship is a discipline and a profession whose practitioners possess (or ought to possess) that special knowledge and expertise described in the LEPU statement.[15]

Given discontinuity in the academic environment, how can we reach for an appropriate and meaningful philosophical definition of librarianship? First, it is wise to look upon conventional and valuable analytic tools, such as task analysis, with some caution. In recent years task analysis has frequently been used in an attempt to distinguish and categorize work in the library. Christianson points out that the study of paraprofessionals in other fields—nursing, social work, education, and mental health—shows that "task analysis is extremely important in using manpower efficiently."[16] Wert cites several studies which identify anywhere from 36 to 1,615 tasks.[17] Zimmerman cites 316 tasks done by catalogers and reference librarians at the Library of Congress.[18] And the University of California's Library Council listed many hundreds of tasks in a study done in 1977.[19] The well-known Illinois task analysis study summarized by Ricking and Booth concludes:

> Once again, it must be emphasized that this study is based on the tasks performed in a specific group of small to medium-sized public libraries, as described in the Phase I document of the Task Analysis Project. No metropolitan public libraries, school, special, college or university libraries were included. While the methodology may be applied to tasks in any library, the model and recommendations will not have universal application.[20]

Canelas has articulated a sound criticism of the Illinois task study:

> Perhaps its greatest weakness is that it does not distinguish between levels of professional performance or clerical performance . . . the categories of tasks are treated as single entities.[21]

Even Ricking and Booth themselves recognize that task analysis has its limitations:

> We learned as we proceeded that we should have started at a different point from the one we used; that the definition of goals must come before the identification of tasks; that tasks derive from programs, programs develop in response to stated goals, stated goals come from the assessment of needs. . . . We came to realize that an understanding of the process is more important than a task list which may result from it; that the methodology, rather than the product, is likely to be of most help in the field.[22]

From this comment and a survey of other literature, we conclude that *it is vital not to be trapped into defining the profession solely via an operational model*, that is, by means of an inventory of specific, observable tasks or job assignments, though such may be helpful if the distinctions described below are maintained. The distinction between academic and support staff goes beyond task analysis and is best defined through an abstract, conceptual model, not via any simplistic inventory, however exhaustive, of tasks, duties and responsibilities with their inevitable areas of overlap or ambiguity. The major reason for caution with the task-oriented approach is that task analysis by itself does not account for the qualitative or conceptual aspect of the "task" being performed by the academic appointee. Task analysis examines only visible, external, operational facets, not the internal framework or intellectual and theoretical foundations for the activity. In defining a truly professional responsibility it is impossible to segregate knowledge, skills, judgments, and "tasks" from the position as a whole, as a gestalt. This gestalt approach is similar to that taken by Wilkinson at the University of Western Ontario who identified four characteristics as the *sine qua non* of all professional positions: (1) basic academic qualifications which guarantee professional expertise in the specialist field of the position, (2) judgment which involves the application of expertise to the reasoned analysis of alternatives in order to determine a preferable course of action, (3) client relationship which involves the librarian as mentor of the patron, (4) voluntary involvement in professional activities through formal external contacts which serves as continuing self-education.[23]

No professional in any field spends one hundred percent of his/her time doing completely professional things: doctors apply Band-Aids,® hold hands, and dole out aspirin. But physicians are judged by the toughest demands that may with confidence be made upon them; the fact that a nurse's aide can put on a Band-Aid® does not make the aide a doctor or a nurse. It is the *upper limits* of the professional's expertise, not the lower limits, that are the criterion. Librarians will have to accept that kind of criterion too; not what one does some of the time, but what one may reasonably be called upon to do is the key.

"Capacity" vs. Position

There is yet another misconception about the academic/nonacademic distinction which needs to be addressed, namely, the idea that different employment series imply an incapacity to perform in another series. All too often classified staff have been given the impression, completely untrue, that they lack the capacity to perform or learn to perform at the "professional" level. Actually, the issue of capacity is irrelevant. The real issue is *position*: How many of what types of employees, that is positions, do we need (and can we afford to pay) to accomplish the work of the university library? It is the *program* of the university and the university library administration which will determine the allocation and distribution of all billets, whether academic or nonacademic. The *program* is the driving force and the budget is the restraining force. Those with capacity or who believe they have the capacity always have the option of applying for programmatically justified academic vacancies on the basis of their current knowledge, skills and abilities, or acquiring the first professional degree (M.L.S.) to enhance their current level of qualifications. This is the apparatus or mechanism by which the "fence" may properly be crossed, no other. Of course, if capacity must be disregarded, then it follows that library management must not confound the issue by assigning professional responsibilities to library assistants or other classified staff, no matter how well "qualified" they may be to perform, a point emphasized by ALA nearly three decades ago.[24] Nor may individual librarians delegate their programmatic responsibilities to nonacademic staff for any reason. (From time to time an argument is heard that it is more important to "get the work done" than to see that it is done by the right category of employee. To be sure, anyone may be called upon to assist in emergencies on a strictly temporary basis. But from the viewpoint of continuing program and position, it is far better that work remain *undone* in order that position justifications remain valid and recruiting be justified. Work that can be "done by anyone" on any occasion does not require professional positions and such positions will not be defensible before personnel reviewing agencies.)

Reaching for a Definition of Professionalism in Librarianship

Doubtless there are innumerable ways to define a professional. Van Rijn has laid the foundation for *job* analysis, a technique that goes far beyond the merely "observable" tasks that flaw task-oriented analyses of professional positions.[25] Asheim and Hilz have struggled with the problem for librarianship and computer programming, respectively.[26,27] But in the context of the discontinuity model it is sufficient to identify those broad responsibilities which will characterize the librarian clearly enough that he/she may be easily distinguished from support staff. One criterion of professional responsibility in librarianship is whether the incumbent may reasonably be expected to conduct intellectual analyses of general problem areas such that the results consist of options, plans, and strategies constituting specific resource allocation recommendations and decisions, that is, Wilkinson's second criterion. A "yes" answer clearly implies an academic and professional responsibility. The generalized problem solving or intellectual aspect of the professional's work within the context of the total discipline of library science is the key element in understanding the respective roles of the professional and the support staff individuals. While the latter make many, many vital decisions on a day-to-day and hour-by-hour basis, *such decisions are qualitatively quite different from those made by academics*. They will likely be of an operational nature and fall within prescribed guidelines or follow procedures predefined by professionals.[28]

What then will be different about the decisions made by professionals? First, decisions made by professionals are related more closely to the *gravity and scope* of a problem than to its frequency. Professional decisions may be expected to fall in the area of *policy*, that is, whether to do something at all, not necessarily how to do it or in what sequence; in the area of *innovative system design*, that is, development of a whole congeries of complexly interacting tasks and procedures; in the area of *program design*, that is, the recommendation or decision to implement a specified series of program elements which support some aspect of the university's teaching, research, or community service, for examples, organization, structure, and management of a major unit in the library, proposals for the creation, dissolution, or combination of units or proposals, for the allocation of certain numbers of other professionals and support staff to a given activity. Second, the professional is expected to operate chiefly at the abstract, intellectual level—comparatively infrequently at the procedural or task level, and such tasks or procedures as are carried out by professionals are likely to be only incidental to or supportive of the main function.[29] The professional also has the requisite educational background, normally the M.L.S., which provides a broad view of the role of the library in society and in the university. Additional degrees, knowledge, or experience will help keep the professional informed on the programmatic needs of the library. The nonprofessional is generally assigned to perform specific tasks or tasks unique to a specific subject area or part of the library, or even tasks specific to one institution or library. This distinction does not operate to prevent non-professional staff from contributing significantly to development of the library's programmatic needs, but such employees cannot be assigned program development as a primary responsibility any more than a teaching assistant can be delegated responsibility for development of curriculum in an academic department.

The above mix of responsibilities may identify the professional too closely with the librarian's administrative or management roles. What about librarians who are not managers, for example, catalogers and reference librarians? Here too, it is necessary to recognize that there is no single, unitary test of professionalism. An individual working alone can be equally as professional as the librarian who directs a large and complex library system. Thus, another component or "test" for professionalism is the extent of involvement in a creative, intellectual enterprise. This might include, for example, devising special cataloging and classification schemas for unique or rare materials, or for the unique academic requirements of an advanced specialized research institute. Other creative activity could comprehend the design and implementation of instructional programs for students and faculty and the provision of advanced reference and research assistance in specialized subjects; developing portions of the collections which require special subject expertise and constant liaison with the faculty; or extensive, in-depth research arising from institional program needs or personal interests. Additional aspects of a librarian's professional work include monitoring graduate students, orienting new faculty to library resources and research tools, and acting as gatekeeper, negotiator or intermediary in respect to the rapidly increasing number of computerized databases. All such work is conducted within the context of the full professional background in library science so that the specialized activity is comprehended within the scope of a gestalt and not merely the implementation of a narrow specialization.

To reach for a meaningful definition of librarianship, a first step is to eschew the simple, exhaustive inventory of duties and responsibilities or housekeeping tasks and procedures as "the solution." The inventory approach merely worsens the problem because the result does not very readily accommodate to changing conditions. (The pitfalls of "list making" are evident in Shaffer's 1968 work where the author compiled approximately a hundred duties and categorized them as professional and nonprofessional. A significant number of his "professional" entries would no longer qualify as such in the 1980s.).

A second step is to strive for generality and flexibility, and to stress the profession's theoretical foundations. As Shaffer has eloquently stated: "Without theory there can be no professional education, and at best the vocation can be no more than a craft practised by skilled individuals who have a charitable attitude towards the people they serve."[30] Thirty years ago Pierce Butler, in a landmark paper on the library profession, complained that "librarians have alway operated with an empirical rather than theoretical attitude toward their problems." He went on to say that "Their techniques are so matter-of-fact that a layman can quickly learn them on the job."[31] That this continuity/discontinuity issue is still with us after three decades should itself be sufficient justification for proper attention to librarianship's theoretical foundations in library school curricula and in the administration of today's academic libraries.

A third step is to stress the idea that librarianship is a full—but unique—component of the intellectual life of the university, different from the professoriate but no less dispensable. Therefore the librarian has a special opportunity and obligation to be creative and responsive in a variety of ways beyond mere service—certainly including teaching, research and publication. It goes without saying that the library administration must support this view and provide opportunity for soundly based, well conceived academic activity by librarians.

A fourth step is to provide for growth and to encourage the librarian's continuing adaptation to change, for example by the expectation of constant involvement in national professional affairs and self-motivated continuing education.

Conclusions

We conclude that librarians directly support a university's academic programs of instruction, research, publication and community service. In fulfilling their programmatic responsibilities librarians analyze problems to formulate options, plans and strategies which result in resource allocation decisions at a variety of levels. Librarians establish program goals and objectives, manage funds for personnel and library materials, select library materials, administer major library service units, and design library systems and procedures. Librarians provide formal and informal bibliographic instruction to undergraduates, graduate students and faculty, and they provide advanced reference assistance and research support to students, faculty and researchers. They participate in creating and administering national and international standard systems for organizing and accessing materials from every country, in every language, and from all time frames. In short, librarians create integrated services and programs which enable the library to support a university's mission and to assist in the direct implementation of its academic programs.

We further conclude that librarianship, like the professoriate, is characterized by discontinuity and that the effective operation of the library as an institution is dependent upon the design, implementation and effective administration of several employment series. Given the variety of employment series within a university, we also conclude that it is essential to distinguish the respective series through carefully prepared definitions and equally essential to administer the distinctions equitably and fairly.

Librarianship has changed radically in the past two decades and will continue to change rapidly under the impact of advancing technology. We need to catch up with the new reality and we need to discard old realities; we need to look forward, not backward. Many who came into the profession twenty or more years ago brought with them a different world-view and different career goals and some have been overtaken by events. The fact is that new technology acts constantly to transfer complex functions downward in the work hierarchy.[32] Even very complex functions—such as cataloging or encoding of bibliographic data—are driven downward to lower levels in the organization. As the profession advances and the work environment changes, some of the duties and responsibilities which are today's professional work may migrate to the level of library specialists, technicians or others, while librarians as the leading professionals in this old/new business of "information processing"—something we've been at for centuries—go on to consider the ever present challenges of new technologies, new needs, and new demands from our clientele. For at the same time that certain functions are being driven downward, *technology is also driving other functions upward*. Some of the upward driven functions will have evolved from earlier professional duties and expectations and some will be altogether new. Hence, we need to abandon any static concept of librarianship as a fixed body of knowledge with a preconceived distribution of tasks, duties and responsibilities. *Librarianship is an evolving profession and must continue to evolve*. A universal hallmark of any profession is adaptability. The pace of change is not even remaining constant—it is quickening. If we cannot respond to the challenges now facing us and cannot adapt to change, then we can be sure that some new institution or service agency will arise in response to public need. Time was when one could glibly say "plus ça change, plus c'est la même chose." A more appropriate apothegm for today might be: "The more things change the more they will *never* be the same."[33]

ACKNOWLEDGEMENTS

In a sense this essay is a collective effort. So many persons have advised and assisted the author that it would be impossible to acknowledge help without the risk of omitting an important name. However, I would be remiss in not thanking specifically several persons without whose aid this work would not have been completed.

I especially wish to thank Margaret Myers, Head of the ALA's Office of Library Personnel Resources who furnished me with a vast amount of source material and who gave me encouragement. Also to be specially thanked are William F. McCoy, chair of the University of California Library Council's Personnel Committee and John Tanno, who represented the Librarians Association of the University of California on that committee. Members of the committee made significant contributions to the work as did Judy Horn, head of the Government Documents department at the Irvine campus of U.C. I sought and received excellent counsel from twelve to fifteen directors of ARL libraries, from the staff of ARL's Office of Management Studies, and the deans of several library schools. All Assistant University Librarians at the Santa Barbara campus of U.C. contributed. Katherine Mawdsley, former president of the Librarians Association of U.C. and Joyce Toscan, current president, contributed indirectly through numerous lengthy discussions.

Special acknowledgement is herewith made to Lester E. Asheim, William Rand Kenan, Jr., Professor of Library Science, University of North Carolina at Chapel Hill, who conscientiously reviewed various versions of this text and permitted many of his suggestions to be directly incorporated. Because Professor Asheim was the principal architect of the American Library Association's policy statement, *Library Education and Personnel Utilization*, his advice and counsel have been especially valued and appreciated.

NOTES

1. See especially Richard M. Dougherty's similar concerns in a discussion of the ALA and the NLA in *Information Hotline*, June 1978, p. 22.

2. The continuity/discontinuity aspect of personnel administration may be more characteristic of the public than the private university library. In two private university libraries known to be well administered, directors reported the problem was either not present or only marginally so, but in several others it stood out prominently. All directors of public university libraries who were consulted were familiar with it.

3. The growth pattern for all large, North American research libraries during this period is essentially identical, so it can be argued that the two phases have affected U.S. and Canadian libraries more or less equally.

4. In this connection it may be worth observing that the need for filing experts in libraries is already disappearing as online catalogs develop and different kinds of talents will be needed for the inverse of filing–retrieval.

5. Pamela Foss, "General Principles of Position Classification." Chicago, ALA/ OLPR/LED/LAD Paper from Preconference on Effective Personnel Utilization: LEPU Guidelines and Principles, June 16, 1977. An excellent and lucid presentation by an expert.

6. The identification of certain intellectual activities with the concept of "production" is certain to induce an emotional response from some, but the validity of the concept cannot be questioned. Even though we pride ourselves in developing the spiritual and the intangible, we continue to count books cataloged, reference questions answered, and total student contact hours. The *fact* of production is evidence of responsiveness to a need and should not confound anyone into thinking that industrial production models apply to libraries and universities.

7. Sandy Bayless, "Librarianship is a Discipline" *Library Journal* 102 (September 1, 1977):1715–1717. Note especially her comments on p. 1717: "If we decide that librarianship is primarily a skill rather than a discipline, a job that is largely a matter of practical experience rather than formal education, then anyone could and should be able to work into a professional position through on the job training."

8. Charles C. Williamson, *Training for Library Service* (New York, Carnegie Corporation, 1923) 165 p.

9. Richard M. Dougherty, "Personnel Needs for Librarianship's Uncertain Future." In: *Academic Libraries by the Year 2000*, Herbert Poole, ed. (New York: Bowker, 1977) p. 112.

10. American Library Association, Committee on Accreditation, *Standards for Accreditation, 1972* (Chicago: ALA 1972) p. 5

11. William Goode, a professor of sociology at Columbia, writing in 1961 did not believe that librarianship was a profession and he foresaw little probability that it could become one. His paper "The Librarian. From Occupation to Profession?" which was severely critical of librarianship, details these stereotypes exquisitely and will not be pleasant reading. It is perhaps the most lucid presentation of the view that it is not a profession. It appears as a chapter in *Seven Questions About Librarianship*, edited by Philip H. Ennis and Howard W. Winger (Chicago: University of Chicago Press, 1962).

12. Complexity of task cannot be a sole criterion by which one distinguishes librarians from support staff. Today, library assistants carry out tasks infinitely more complex than those done by catalogers, for example, a generation ago. One need only look at the assistants' work with the MARC format and input to the bibliographic networks. But complexity of work in and of itself does not make them librarians, for the whole of librarianship itself has become correspondingly more complex and the work of support staff remains but a component or subset of the totality.

13. ALA Office of Library Personnel Resources, *Library Education and Personnel Utilization. A Statement of Policy Adopted by the Council of the American Library Association, June 30, 1970* (Chicago: ALA 1970) 8 p.

14. National Librarians Association, Certification Standards Committee, *Draft Position Paper* (May 1979) 11 p. See page 11, item 6.2 which is taken verbatim from *LEPU.*

15. Goode's severe critique may well be applied against this claim, but his well-taken points would have to be addressed in another study. Besides, twenty years have elapsed

since his paper and an entirely new review is in order. Compare Asheim's recent paper, "Librarians as Professionals," in *Library Trends* 27 (Winter 1979):225–257.

16. Elin Christianson, *Paraprofessional and Nonprofessional Staff in Special Libraries* (New York: Special Libraries Association, 1973) 69 p. (SLA State-of-the-Art Review, no. 2). See especially pp. 46–51, "Paraprofessionals in Other Fields."

17. Lucille M. Wert, "The MLS and Performance: What We Know to Date." Typescript of paper prepared for 1978 ALA Annual Conference, OLPR Program: "Minimum Qualifications for Librarians."

18. Glen A. Zimmerman. "Job Validation at the Library of Congress." Paper presented at the ALA Annual Conference, OLPR Program: "Minimum Qualifications for Librarians." Chicago, June 27, 1978.

19. University of California Library Council, Personnel Committee, *Report of the Personnel Committee on the Investigation of the Library Assistant Series*, October 3, 1977. See the 80-page Appendix IV, "Duties Assigned to Staff Personnel in the Libraries of the University of California."

20. Myrl Ricking and Robert E. Booth, *Personnel Utilization in Libraries—A Systems Approach* (Chicago: ALA, 1974) 152 p.

21. Dale B. Canelas, "Position Classification in Libraries and an Introduction to the *Library Education and Personnel Utilization Policy*." Paper prepared for the ALA conference, June 1977.

22. Ricking and Booth, *Personnel Utilization in Libraries—A Systems Approach*, pp. vii–ix.

23. John Wilkinson, Kenneth Plate and Robert Lee, "A Matrix Approach to Position Classification" *College & Research Libraries* 36 (Sept. 1975):357–363.

24. ALA Board on Personnel Administration, Subcommittee on Job Analysis Manual and Classification and Pay Plan Manual, *Position Classification and Salary Administration in Libraries* (Chicago: ALA, 1951) 81 p. See especially p. 46: "Unless their actual duties change, they must remain in the grade of their present positions, no matter how high their qualifications are."

25. Paul van Rijn, *Job Analysis for Selection: An Overview*. Washington, US Office of Personnel Management, Staffing Services Group, 1979. (Personnel Research & Development Center, Professional Series, 79–2). 22 p.

26. Lester Asheim, "Librarians as Professionals." *Library Trends* 27 (Winter 1979):225–257.

27. D. J. Hiltz, "Programmers and Analysts Are Not Professionals." *Datamation* (August 1978) pp. 199–202.

28. As the library gets deeper into computer applications an increasing amount of production work will attain a high order of complexity and will require highly qualified, highly trained and appropriately compensated classified personnel. But this work will nevertheless continue to be of different character from that done by librarians. Of course the whole cadre of classified personnel in this environment will require upgrading of skills and classification as well as the development of a specific career ladder.

29. For example, when a professional searches a card catalog, printed bibliography or computerized data base, it cannot be claimed that such activity is "the same" as searching done by support staff for the purpose, goal, scope and intent of the "same" physical activity will be quite different, and so will the search process.

30. Dale Eugene Shaffer, *The Maturity of Librarianship as a Profession* (Metuchen N.J.: Scarecrow, 1968) p. 86.

31. Pierce Butler, "Librarianship as a Profession" *Library Quarterly* 21 (October 1951):245.

32. Allen B. Veaner, "Management and Technology." *IFLA Journal* 7 (1981):32–37.

33. This statement is taken from the cover design of a special issue of *Datamation* devoted to major transitions in the data processing world, the issue for November 15, 1978, vol. 24, no. 12.

REFERENCES

ALA Board on Personnel Administration. Subcommittee on Analysis of Library Duties. *Descriptive List of Professional and Nonprofessional Duties in Libraries.* Chicago, ALA, 1948. 75 p.

ALA Board on Personnel Administration. Subcommittee on Personnel Organization and Procedure. *Personnel Organization and Procedure: A Manual Suggested for Use in College and University Libraries.* Chicago, ALA, 1952. 57 p.

American Library Association, Office for Library Personnel Resources, Minimum Qualifications for Librarians Task Force. "Minimum Qualifications for Librarians: What are the Issues?" Chicago, ALA, Revised, July 1979. 6 p.

Association of Research Libraries. Systems and Procedures Exchange Center. *Paraprofessionals in ARL Libraries.* SPEC Kit No. 21, October, 1975.

Association of Research Libraries. Systems and Procedures Exchange Center. *Personnel Classification Schemes and Job Descriptions.* SPEC Kit No. 7, May 1974.

Berry, John. "The Two 'Professions'". *Library Journal* 102 (September 1, 1977):1699.

Blume, Julie. "Assuring Professional Competence Through Education or Examination: A Selective Bibliography." Chicago, ALA/OLPR and Standing Committee on Library Education, 1978. 103 entries; annotated.

Cottam, Keith. "Minimum Qualifications and the Law: The Issue Ticks Away for Librarians." *American Libraries* 11 (May 1980):280–281.

Crowe, Jr., William J. "A Select Bibliography of Materials Relating to Position Classification in Libraries." Prepared for the ALA/OLPR/LED/LAD Preconference on Effective Personnel Utilization: LEPU Guidelines and Principles. Detroit, June 16, 1977. 9 p.

Estabrook, Leigh, and Blumenthal, Thomas. "The Impact of Social Change in the Library: A Literature Review." Chicago, ALA, 1977.

Foss, Pamela. "Position Classification Bibliography." June 16, 1977. Annotated; companion to Ms. Foss's paper on the subject. See footnote 5.

Galvin, Thomas J., et al. "The New Role of Librarians as Professionals: A Literature Review." Chicago, ALA, 1977.

Krueger, Donald, ed. "Bibliography on professionalism." *The National Librarian* 3 (4) (November 1978):7–8. A bibliography on professionalism is a regular feature of this newsletter.

Mahmoodi, Suzanne H. "Identification of Competencies for Librarians Serving Public Service Functions in Public Libraries." Ph.D. dissertation, University of Minnesota, 1978.

Neill, Samuel D. "Who Needs to Go to Graduate Library School?" *Journal of Education for Librarianship*, 13 (Spring 1973):212–225.

Schiller, Anita. "Women in Librarianship." *Advances in Librarianship* 4 (1974):103–141.

Sparks, C. Paul. "Job Analysis Bibliography." Exxon Company, Houston, Texas, 1979. Reprinted with permission by American Library Association. 19 p. Most of the 219 items are less than ten years old and a substantial number date from 1978–79.

Taylor, Robert S. "Reminiscing About the Future: Professional Education and the Information Environment." *Library Journal* 104 (September 15, 1979):1871–75.

ARCHIBALD CARY COOLIDGE AND "CIVILIZATION'S DIARY":
BUILDING THE HARVARD UNIVERSITY LIBRARY

Robert F. Byrnes

Archibald Cary Coolidge helped transform Harvard University from a small New England college into one of the great universities of the world when he was a member of the Harvard faculty from 1893 until his death in January 1928. An imaginative and constructive teacher of undergraduates, director of graduate studies, scholar, and editor, Coolidge also helped make the Harvard University Library one of the finest university systems and collections in the world, one which has served as a model for other American academic institutions. This achievement also demonstrates that Coolidge was a major contributor to the expansion and transformation of higher education in the United States in the years following 1880.

Advances in Library Administration and Organization, volume 1, pages 21–42
Copyright © 1982 by JAI PRESS INC.
ISBN: 0-89232-213-6

Coolidge lived from the end of the Civil War until just before the depression of 1929. Born into a prosperous Beacon Hill family, proud of its origins in the histories of the commonwealths of Massachusetts and of Virginia, Coolidge benefited from leisurely travel as a youngster and throughout his life, and early mastery of French, Italian, and German and then of other languages, beginning with Russian. He enjoyed a Harvard undergraduate education and six years of graduate study in France and Germany and travels throughout Europe and around the world before he joined the Harvard Department of History as an instructor in the fall of 1893.

At Harvard, the center of Coolidge's life, activity, and influence, his emphasis upon widening the university's horizons and upon quality helped change the Department of History from one that played a secondary role in the university into one that enjoyed a golden age and constituted for some years the outstanding group of scholars in history in the United States. His policies and standards affected other areas of the university as well, especially those involved in instruction concerning other parts of the world and in foreign languages. Among a stellar group of scholars he was the one most responsible, under Presidents Charles W. Eliot and A. Lawrence Lowell, for bringing Harvard into touch with the rest of the world. The Eliot and Lowell years made the university part of "the great globe itself" and transformed Harvard from a New England college into a model or pacemaker for other institutions. The Harvard emphases upon intellectual quality and upon study of the universe set standards that other American universities emulated.

In utilizing fully his wealth and family position, this creative man was in many ways a predecessor of the great foundations in stimulating change in American universities. He played the role of Johnny Appleseed by training approximately fifty young men who helped introduce the history of Western civilization as the basic freshman history course. He launched research and instruction in modern history and in the history of other countries and cultures at Harvard and, through those whom he trained, in colleges and universities across the country. Indeed, his definition of history spread like an infectious disease as his graduates distributed themselves throughout the United States, to teach about Russia, Latin America, China, Eastern Europe, and the Middle East. Some of those he trained became "theologians," teachers who were also productive research scholars, who trained young professional historians in such major institutions as the University of Illinois, the University of California at Berkeley, and Stanford University. Others became "parish priests" and instructed undergraduates in large and small colleges across the land.

Coolidge launched this effort to modernize the university just when the war with Spain made the United States an important world state and created new responsibilities for its leaders. His work in identifying and educating young men for work in the Department of State assisted significantly in the creation of a professional Foreign Service. The research and advisory services he and those whom he trained performed after the United States entered World War I helped lessen confusion at the peace conference in Paris. The work of scholars in Washington and in Paris demonstrated to government officials the quality of mind scholars could bring to analysis of contemporary international problems. They also helped define the relationship between government and the academic community by showing that professors must function as independent analysts and critics when they assisted in times of national emergency.

Coolidge's work in The Inquiry and in the American Commission to Negotiate Peace from 1917 to 1919 enlivened and deepened the interest of American historians concerning the need to expand attention to other peoples and to the outside world. It also led to his most signal effort to increase knowledge and understanding of the world and of international politics beyond the university, a function he had begun the year he joined the Harvard faculty, when he first wrote for the *Nation*. As editor of *Foreign Affairs* during its first six years, 1922–1928, he helped make it the most influential American journal on international politics.

One of Coolidge's most significant contributions to Harvard and to American higher education was his leadership in transforming the Harvard University Library into one of the best organized for scholars and students as well as one of the great libraries of the world. Books fascinated him. Bookstores everywhere attracted his careful study. Throughout his career, browsing among new books or examining volumes on subjects in which he was interested provided special pleasure and produced new ideas and inspiration. Whether in Tomsk or in Budapest, he would visit the library to examine its physical plant, collections, and catalogue system. The differences his travels in Europe in the 1880s and 1890s revealed between the Bibliothèque Nationale, the Prussian State Library in Berlin, and the crowded old library in the Yard led him to concentrate on that part of Harvard's foundations as soon as he joined the faculty in 1893. Growing interest in other peoples and in international affairs increased his determination to expand the university's book collection.

On a trip around the world in 1906 he wrote long letters from Calcutta and Bombay to his history colleague, Charles H. Haskins, about his vision of a great Harvard library. These missives provided detailed comments on more than a dozen areas on which the university should make ''a respectable showing.'' Harvard was particularly weak in modern European history and possessed practically no primary documents for the study of world affairs. He outlined steps the library should take at his expense to enlarge its French collection and reorganize its classification system, "a harmless, if futile, whim."[1] From the time he was appointed at Harvard but especially after 1910 when he became director of the library, it was a central cause. Every aspect of its work interested him. It was always in his mind, whether he was in Cracow or in Kenya, and he lavished energy, funds, and creativity upon it. It gave him a sense of community that he cherished. Some colleagues observed that it occupied the place that families filled in their lives and that they might properly term it "the Harvard Coolidge Library." When Harvard awarded him an honorary degree in 1916, President Lowell declared that "every colleague owes [him] a debt of gratitude as foremost among living administrators of libraries for scholars."

For Coolidge, a library was "not a charnel house filled with the bones of dead ideas, but rather a garden in which they might be made to germinate and grow and bear fruit, each after its kind."[2] He urged students to read widely and showed them through the library. Freshmen learned they should consider the library a cathedral from which to draw inspiration throughout their lives.

In his view, every library's first and most basic problem was to define its public and to meet its readers' needs in space, facilities, staff, and collection. Earlier than most scholar librarians, he realized that each library has a different purpose from every other library, and that these goals were constantly changing. For an educational institution with aspirations for eminence, the library was the indispensable base. While "a library does not make a university, a great university today cannot exist without a good library of its own or within reach."[3]

Travel and studies persuaded him that Harvard enjoyed a splendid opportunity to emerge as *the* university in the United States and to become one "with the great schools of the old world." Ambitions for Harvard and its library were especially high because "more is expected of the first university in America. It is there that every man should naturally turn first." Harvard must therefore accept the leadership and burden of greatness in library collections as well as in faculty and establish standards for other American universities to follow.[4] At the dedication on June 24, 1915 of Widener Library, Coolidge defined his goals:

> "We aim to make the library the glory of Harvard, to have it add to the fame and the influence of the university, and to constitute one of the chief attractions to all connected with the institution, whether as teachers or as students." He went on to hope that "the ever increasing value of its collections and the opportunities for the use of them will draw scholars from near and far and send them back enthusiastic over what they have found and grateful to the name of Harvard."[5]

When Lowell became president in 1909 the library constituted a critical problem. Moreover, he had learned as a member of the faculty that the then librarian, William Coolidge Lane, a gentle, courteous, and neat antiquarian, lacked the vision, force, and influence with the faculty to direct the necessary changes. The system was thoroughly disorganized, central in theory, but one in which the librarian in practice had little influence over the eleven department and school libraries. The main building, Gore, was so crowded even in 1894 that 15,000 volumes were stored in the basement of the chapel. At the turn of the century, President Eliot considered discarding infrequently used volumes rather than seeking space and money for storage. In 1910 the library had 543,000 volumes crammed in every conceivable corner of the building, and 50,000 volumes were stored elsewhere. The faculty had no studies, the library provided no reading rooms for undergraduate or graduate students, and the stacks constituted a serious fire hazard.

The classification system and the catalogue represented even more serious problems. Several systems of cataloguing had developed since the Civil War, and the library had no university union catalogue. Coolidge estimated that at least 75,000 volumes were not in the public catalogue and that 200,000 were unclassified or defectively classified. The subject catalogue was disorganized and fundamentally useless. The library cards were smaller than those that the Library of Congress and the John Crerar Library had adopted in 1901, which were becoming standard throughout the country. Thus, the library needed a unified system of classification and cataloguing, a gigantic program to catalogue or re-catalogue thousands of volumes, and a mammoth effort to convert its library cards into the same size as those of the Library of Congress.[6]

The book collection, Coolidge's principal concern, had tripled in thirty-five years. Still, the library in 1910 had only $31,500 for purchasing and binding books, of which the university contributed only $18,000. Moreover, the total expended for administration was about $80,000, of which less than $25,000 was for salaries. The Boston Public Library at that time spent more than eight times as much as Harvard on staff salaries.[7]

Lowell in November 1909 named Coolidge chairman of the Library Council, founded in 1867 to establish general library policy, which consisted of the president, the librarian, and six faculty members appointed by the Corporation at the president's recommendation. Coolidge, who had become a member of the Council in 1908, was an ideal appointment, not only because of contributions he had made to improving the library in the previous fifteen years, but also because of his enthusiastic interest in the library and his knowledge of other institutions. His admiration for German libraries was great, and his contributions at Harvard reflected much he had learned about purpose and organization there. Lowell especially valued his high standing in the faculty and among alumni, crucial because the sensitive and alert faculty might resist change, and his willingness to accept responsibility and not bother the president with minor questions.

Coolidge accepted appointment under conditions that Lowell quickly granted, beginning with administrative power over the Harvard College Library and supervisory authority over the university's other libraries. Lowell dropped Lane from the Council and added particularly able faculty members. He also consented that the Corporation would appoint a Library Council secretary, whom Coolidge would nominate and pay. Finally, Coolidge resigned as chairman of the Department of History and reduced his teaching obligations to one course and one seminar each year. Lowell in turn awarded the department an additional appointment, Robert H. Lord, in Russian and German history.

The new chairman quickly demonstrated vision and vigorous administrative ability. After he presented a comprehensive analysis "looking back and ahead" for the library at the first meeting he chaired, in January 1910, the Council persuaded Lowell and the Corporation to authorize a management review of the library's organization and administration. Even before this review had been completed, in November 1910, Coolidge persuaded Lowell to name him Director of the Harvard University Library in order to increase his nominal authority over the other libraries, particularly those of the Law School and the School of Medicine, which cherished their independent positions. The Law School, for example, resisted transferring books that had no relationship to law from its collection and sought to sell these volumes to the College. In relations with these libraries, Coolidge demonstrated such tact that their councils soon accepted him as a member. The steady improvement of the library system and the quantities of books purchased for each library system persuaded all that a federal system was useful and created a spirit of local self-government within the system that made the Harvard arrangement one of the marvels and models of the library world. When he died, the faculties of the Schools of Law and Medicine expressed the deepest and warmest appreciation of his services. The Medical School Library Committee called him "the University type of a Professor" and "a refreshing link" with Cambridge.[8]

Within the library administration itself, Coolidge was "a generous and thoughtful commanding officer." The appointment at first affronted some professional librarians, including Lane, but good sense and dedication soon overcame this resentment. The staff learned that "he cared more for this library than anything else in the world."[9] He not only provided vision and leadership but also encouraged teamwork and shared responsibility, from discussing major policies to moving books from the old library to the new. These qualities, his devotion to the library, buoyant enthusiasm, and visible satisfaction from seeing the collection grow and the system improve helped stimulate colleagues throughout the library to ever greater effectiveness.

Coolidge inherited and selected able assistants and gave them full support and independence. Refusing to pose as a professional librarian, he attended only one American Library Association annual meeting, that in nearby Swampscott in June 1921. There a talk on "The Objects of Cataloguing," a paper of considerable sense and erudition, increased the respect professional librarians had for him.[10]

Coolidge identified space, the catalogue and classification system, and the collection as the major elements that needed attention. He worked throughout his years as director on these three issues, but concentrated the first five years on establishing a simple classification system and reforming the catalogue, fundamental but essentially dull chores which he considered the most controversial aspects of the changes introduced.

The conviction that a library catalogue "takes an honorable place among the agencies that contribute to the progress of our civilization" was central to his system of priorities. Experience indicated that most subject catalogues were too complicated, that faculty members made little use of them because they relied instead on bibliographies and professional journals, and that simplicity and good sense should serve as guidelines. Establishing an effective but simple classification system, on parts of which he had worked since 1894, he benefited from the work Leo Wiener had done when cataloguing the first collection of books Coolidge had purchased on Russia in the 1890s and from the system which Walter Lichtenstein and other graduate students had established for the publications on Germany that Coolidge had given the university after 1903. The director went through the catalogue slowly and patiently with staff members and graduate students as they created the new system. The tasks of reclassification, creation of a formal dictionary union catalogue, and making both the public and the official catalogues complete were basically finished before the move into Widener Library in 1915, but the work continued after Coolidge's death. Indeed, one of his very last letters in December 1927 was to an assistant librarian about the system of classifying books on Russia before and after 1917.

The decision that most impressed those who used the library was that in 1910 to introduce the same size cards as the Library of Congress had adopted in 1901. In his first year as director, Harvard purchased and filed 470,000 copies of Library of Congress cards and 70,000 cards from the John Crerar Library. By 1915 the staff had inserted the new cards, had punched and inserted 1,500,000 old Harvard Library cards into the new catalogue, and had begun the tedious work of typing and printing copies of the old cards. Coolidge had copies printed of the more important of the small Harvard College Library cards for which the Library of Congress had no card, persuaded twenty-four other libraries to subscribe to this series, and defrayed all costs that the consortium did not meet. He also paid for typing cards for titles that were not printed. By August 1913, 121,000 titles and perhaps 360,000 cards had been printed and inserted into the catalogue. This operation continued even after Coolidge's death because of the vast number of titles involved.[11]

In short, Coolidge reorganized the classification system and the catalogue of the Harvard University Library, established a union catalogue, provided it the same size card as that of the Library of Congress and other major libraries in the United States, and organized a base on which the staff could manage the catalogue's growth. These central improvements helped lay the foundations on which the library became such a useful tool for students and scholars.

His interest in building the collections was as natural as his concern for the catalogue was remarkable. Acquisitions policy rested on several important principles. First, the library should be designed to serve "today's students and tomorrow's scholars." The university should create a library collection and faculty before establishing an instructional program, particularly a graduate program: "every venture into a new area of scholarship and teaching has to be backed up with library materials."[12] The university should establish and follow a careful system of priorities in purchasing books. Its other obligations and the costs involved persuaded him that it should purchase and catalogue all materials regularly available for instruction in English and other Western languages. Donors, friends, and alumni should provide research materials for graduate programs, especially material on new areas or fields of study and in foreign languages. Coolidge even discouraged donors from contributing expensive rare books until late in his life, although he gratefully welcomed all collections, because rare books occupied a low priority for him. Special collections, on the other hand, "constitute the strength and glory of a great library."

Second, Coolidge appreciated that he was enlarging Harvard's collections at a most opportune time. He felt a permanent sense of urgency concerning purchase of materials and adopted the principle, "Buy first, and find the money afterwards." The university should obtain all the books it could, because "there never will be so favorable a time again" and delay would only increase the magnitude of the problem in later years. He sometimes envisioned "an unending stream pouring down in almost terrifying waves of knowledge upon the library shelves from every nation of the globe."[13]

Finally, Coolidge believed that libraries should cooperate in purchasing books in new fields of study. Harvard should remain the preeminent institution with the finest library, but he was eager to work with other institutions for the common welfare, as in printing the Harvard University Library cards and in creating a National Union Catalogue in the Library of Congress. He advised the University of Chicago and Yale University concerning the strengths and weaknesses of the approaches that Harvard had adopted. He invited other institutions to join Harvard in financing an agent to purchase books in Portugal and Spain in 1911 and 1912 and throughout Latin America in 1914 and 1915, and he was generous and understanding in dividing the volumes purchased.[14]

In 1911 Ernest C. Richardson, librarian of Princeton University, published the *Union List of Collections on European History in American Libraries*, which listed the published series of documents on European history and identified American institutions that possessed full or partial sets of each series. Coolidge discovered that Harvard had somewhat more than sixty percent of these sets, sent Lichtenstein to Europe to acquire full series of those it lacked, and increased Harvard's holdings from 1,267 to about 1,900 of the 2,205 sets that Richardson had identified. Coolidge forwarded to Richardson a list of the errors Lichtenstein had discovered in his tour so that the second edition would be even more accurate and helpful than the first. He then urged American librarians to assist in publishing that edition.

In addition, Coolidge and a number of wealthy alumni were generous contributors to the expensive effort involved in compiling *The Union List of Serials in the United States and Canada*, "by far the most important cooperative undertaking which has been produced by American libraries." Richardson proposed this in 1913, work began in 1922, and the first edition appeared in 1927. This immense volume (1,588 pages) listed the 75,000 serial publications in the world and identified the issues or numbers available in each American library. Few volumes are of more value to scholars in the humanities and social sciences than this and its later editions.[15]

Like Alfred North Whitehead, Coolidge believed that the university should study the universe and that the library collection was the foundation for such research. He demonstrated uncanny insight in identifying the principal areas of study on which future scholars would focus interest. He was not only alert in identifying these needs but was perceptive and rigorous in locating and obtaining materials. Wherever he was, he sought books, investigated bookstores, and talked with scholars about private collections, using his thorough knowledge of the Harvard library to help complete gaps. As visiting professor in Paris in 1906–1907 and in Berlin in 1913–1914, he purchased volumes in French and German history. While in Vienna for five months in 1919 for the American Commission to Negotiate the Peace, he managed to acquire 4,000 volumes on the history of

Central and Eastern Europe. Similarly, his "chief amusement" in Moscow in 1921-1922 for the American Relief Administration was purchasing books, including 1,000 volumes on Russian law and 2,500 volumes on the theater. Lucius Beebe has recorded the unfounded legend that Coolidge rushed to Budapest to purchase 50,000 volumes when Bela Kun seized power in 1919 and decided to sell the major libraries.[16]

Coolidge's first concerns were the Slavic and Balkan fields, where Harvard acquired a leadership it has never lost among American universities. When he returned to Cambridge in 1893, the university had fewer than 2,000 volumes on Russia, and he was the only faculty member who could read Russian. Harvard was not unique then: the Library of Congress in 1901 had 569 volumes in Russian and 97 volumes in Polish, plus uncatalogued volumes the Smithsonian Institution had obtained through exchanges. In 1907 a Krasnoyarsk businessmen, Gennadi V. Yudin, sold the Library of Congress 80,000 volumes in five hundred crates at a low price as a step toward closer relations between Russia and the United States and a contribution to "the world of science." The Library of Congress established the Slavic and Central European Division as an acquisition, reference, and bibliographic center only in 1951, and it did not catalogue these volumes until the 1950s and 1960s.[17]

Similarly, the great days of the Slavic collection of the New York Public Library lay ahead. This library had 1,300 volumes on Russia in 1889, when it founded the Slavonic Division in response to a petition hundreds of recent immigrants from Russia had signed. It did not grow substantially until Avrahm Yarmolinsky was appointed chief in 1918 (he served until 1955). Its heart lay in the 9,000 volumes Yarmolinsky purchased in the Soviet Union and the 700 volumes he acquired in Poland on a trip from April 1923 through September 1924, thirty years after Coolidge had begun to build the Harvard collection.[18]

The Hoover Institution began its library in 1919, when Herbert Hoover gave Professor Ephraim D. Adams of the Stanford University Department of History $50,000 to purchase books, documents, journals, and newspapers in Western Europe. Hoover persuaded General John J. Pershing to help Adams by providing fifteen soldiers who had had academic experience. In this way, using food ships returning empty to the United States for transportation, Adams began the Hoover collection on European history and on war and revolution. The collection grew rapidly in the 1920s, largely because of the work of Golder when he was in Russia with the American Relief Administration.[19]

The entire Slavic section of the Harrassowitz bookstore in Leipzig, which he visited on his way to Siberia in 1895, was Coolidge's first gift of books to the Harvard Library. This contained 1,371 titles, at a time when Harvard possessed about that number of volumes in Slavic history and added a total of about 15,000 volumes a year to its holdings. Coolidge presented these books to the university, helped create a catalogue classification system, and employed Wiener to catalogue the volumes. The following year he added 415 volumes and 180 pamphlets on Russia. In 1899 he began the Polish collection with a gift of 300 volumes. The next year he purchased the Alexander Lombardini collection in Slovak history and literature, which Wiener had discovered on a trip to eastern Europe. Coolidge had begun to purchase books on Slovak history in the 1890s and this addition of 123 volumes and 1,567 pamphlets gave Harvard a collection even in the 1950s "without parallel on this side of the Atlantic and one that could almost certainly never be assembled again." In 1969 this purchase constituted about twenty percent of Harvard's collection on Slovakia.[20]

By 1901 Harvard had 6,100 volumes on Russia and the Balkans. Coolidge continued to add collections, the literature of the Social Revolutionaries and the Nihilists, the nineteenth-century "thick journals," the records of the Duma, Government publications, volumes of railroad statistics, law and theatre, and art. Late in life he began to direct attention to Poland and then to Czechoslovakia, which he had virtually ignored while concentrating upon Russia. Until he died, he purchased and paid for cataloguing virtually all volumes that the university acquired in the Slavic field. Almost all the 30,000 volumes in Harvard's Slavic collection in 1934 were Coolidge gifts.[21]

As in the Department of History, where the course on the Eastern Question followed that introduced on Russia, interest in the collection on the Balkans and the Near East followed that in Russia. These purchases began in 1899, when he and his father purchasd 445 volumes from the library of Charles Schefer in Paris on relations between Turkey and Europe in the sixteenth and seventeenth centuries. The following year Coolidge, his father, and friends together gave the university the Paris library of Count Paul Riant, 7,649 volumes of chronicles and other sources and 1,200 pamphlets on the Crusades and the Latin East. This collection cost $10,735, of which Coolidge contributed $3,750. It was then "the most valuable which the Library has ever received" and constituted a fourth of the volumes Harvard acquired in 1900. Within two decades, three Coolidge students, Theodore F. Jones, Lichtenstein, and Albert H. Lybyer, completed theses on Ottoman history based on the Schefer and Riant collections and John K. Wright one on geographical knowledge during the time of the crusades.[22]

When Coolidge died in 1928 the Harvard collection on the Ottoman Empire consisted of 7,000 volumes. Most of these were in English, but in 1915 Coolidge began to purchase books in Turkish and Arabic and to create a separate catalogue for them and for volumes in Persian. Harvard's collection in 1960 was "the most complete and valuable collection in the United States of western language books on Ottoman history and literature."[23]

Graduate study and travel in Germany in the 1880s and 1890s naturally gave Coolidge a profound interest in the history of that country and of its immediate neighbors. In 1903, when Harvard had about 1,000 volumes on German history, he promised to add at least 10,000 volumes in honor of the visit of Prince Henry of Prussia to Harvard and of the opening of the Germanic Museum (now the Busch-Reisinger Museum of Germanic Culture). This effort "to make Harvard a center for study of all that is highest and noblest in German civilization" began with the purchase of the private library of Professor Konrad von Maurer in Munich, a collection of 2,700 volumes and 2,900 pamphlets largely on the history of Bavaria and the Rhineland. He then gave employment and responsibility to Lichtenstein, who worked for twelve years at Coolidge's expense purchasing and cataloguing Slavic, West European, and Latin American volumes. After concluding that having a purchasing agent in Europe would be sensible, Coolidge sent Lichtenstein to Germany to complete the Hohenzollern collection and to buy books in Scandinavian, Dutch, and Swiss history. In fourteen months this remarkable young man obtained 11,000 volumes from three hundred bookstores in Germany and Central Europe for only $8,622. Coolidge then appointed him honorary Curator of the Hohenzollern Collection, a post he held until 1919. As assistant in charge of European collections, he established a classification system for these volumes and helped catalogue them. The two men then transferred their knowledge of classification to the material Coolidge and others were purchasing on British, French, and Italian history.[24]

Coolidge rejected Lichtenstein's suggestion that Harvard employ a permanent purchasing agent on the continent. However, Lichtenstein made other prolonged trips to Europe and one through Latin America to purchase books, on all of which Coolidge paid his salary and travel expenses. He accepted appointment in 1908 as Librarian and Associate Professor of History at Northwestern University, but spent most of the period through 1914 on leave from Northwestern working for Harvard or for a consortium of university libraries that Coolidge had assembled.[25]

Harvard by 1914 possessed almost all the German historical periodicals and its library was second only to the Prussian State Library in Berlin on German history and culture. These materials naturally included many on Germany's neighbors, especially the Netherlands and Switzerland. Coolidge devoted much time and energy in the first decade of the twentieth century trying to persuade the Iselins and other American families of Swiss origin to contribute to a Swiss collection. In the 1920s he sought to induce Edward Bok and others of Dutch descent to give $100,000 toward a collection in Dutch history in honor of John Lothrop Motley, who graduated from Harvard in 1831. Scandinavia fascinated him throughout his life, and he named Henry Goddard Leach, one of his History 1 discussion leaders and a leading spirit of the American-Scandinavian Foundation for thirty-five years, curator of Scandinavian History and Literature. These endeavors were not notably successful, but the university's resources on Switzerland and the Netherlands did grow because of his purchases. The American-Scandinavian Foundation used the Harvard Library in 1921 when it selected the 500 most important books in English by Scandinavians and about Scandinavia.[26]

France was as close to Coolidge's interests as Germany. In 1906 he gave the university $1,000 as a matching grant for works on French local history. The following year he purchased a splendid collection of 165 newspapers, 10,000 volumes, and 30,000 pamphlets on the French Revolution from Count Alfred Boulay de la Meurthe. Later he gave other volumes on French poetry. In 1931 some of his friends purchased the library of Professor Alphonse Aulard, 3,500 volumes and pamphlets on the French Revolution, as a gift in his memory.[27]

From Germany and France Coolidge moved to the Iberian countries and Latin America. In 1911 he purchased the library of Marquis de Olivart on Spanish history, 8,000 titles particularly strong in law and international law for only $11,500, although he had expected to pay $25,000. He began on Portugal in 1923 by persuading a neighbor and student in the class of 1906, Ambassador John B. Stetson, Jr., whose stepfather was a Portuguese nobleman, to serve as honorary curator to the Portuguese collection, a position he filled actively for thirty years.[28]

Latin America greatly interested him. From 1903 through 1908 he employed another graduate student, Hiram Bingham, later professor at Yale and Senator from Connecticut, as curator of the Latin American collection. When Bingham joined the Yale faculty and seemed determined to build a strong Latin American collection, Harvard decided to grant that area a low priority. However, when Coolidge visited Chile in 1908–1909 as representative of Harvard and the United States to the First Pan-American Scientific Congress, he and his then secretary, Clarence L. Hay, Harvard 1908, acquired for $5,505 the 4,000-volume private library of Louis Montt, the national librarian of Chile. This collection was especially strong on Chile, Peru, and Argentina.

Later, when Bingham demonstrated more interest in exploration than in enlarging the Yale Library, Coolidge sent Lichtenstein through Latin America for fourteen months on a trip from which Harvard, Yale, and other universities benefited. Lichenstein purchased about 9,000 volumes for Harvard at a total cost of slightly more than $17,000. Harvard at that time had the strongest Latin American collection in the United States, and its Law School became "the only place in the world which has a complete collection of the codes and statutory laws of all the independent South American states."[29]

Because of his travels and of his family's long interest in Asia, China, Japan, and Siam also attracted his attention. By 1910, largely through purchases he and his father had made, the library had 1,000 books on China and was "perhaps the best working library outside of Washington." His brother Harold was generous after 1909, contributing annually to the Chinese and Japanese collection. When Edward Henry Strobel, Harvard 1877, died in January 1908 after six years as adviser to the King of Siam, Coolidge persuaded the King and other officials to give $2,000 for books on Siam. The following year, he inspired Strobel's Harvard class to establish a library fund for world politics in his memory. Coolidge added a specialist for Eastern Asia to the library staff in 1927, when Harvard had 4,526 volumes in Chinese and 1,668 in Japanese. His will provided the library $200,000 and the residual sum after his specific bequests primarily for "the purchase of works on European, Asiatic, and African history and government, or works descriptive of the political and economic conditions of the people of those continents."[30]

The United States was not neglected. Coolidge worked closely with Frederick Jackson Turner and Mrs. Alice Hooper in creating the Harvard Commission on Western History as a memorial to her father, Charles Elliott Perkins, who had built the Chicago, Burlington, and Quincy Railroad. This was active from 1911 until 1920, with funds Mrs. Hooper contributed annually, and bought more than 1,000 books on Western history. Coolidge provided a room in Widener Library for the Western collection, appointed an archivist for it, sent him to Salt Lake City in 1914 to purchase a collection on the Mormons, and encouraged alumni, particularly those in the West, to contribute materials and funds. However, Turner was not an aggressive supporter of this drive. Lowell feared it alienated western institutions and understood too late that it might increase interest in the university among western alumni. Finally, the war concentrated American concerns on other parts of the world, so this program waned in Turner's last years at Harvard. However, Turner and Mrs. Hooper both recognized that Coolidge was one member of the Harvard faculty "whose horizon was not limited to his own region." Indeed, Mrs. Hooper was convinced that he deserved much of the credit for transforming Harvard into a major institution that Eliot and Lowell ordinarily received.[31].

It is difficult to determine the magnitude of Coolidge's imaginative collecting and benefactions before his final bequest, because so many gifts were discreet, even anonymous. For example, in 1905, he quietly organized a small group of friends of Harvard and of Professor Charles

Eliot Norton to purchase Norton's library for the university for $15,000. His contributions to the library approximately equalled his salary from 1893 through 1928. He bestowed a total of more than $100,000 for the purchase of books alone. In his last three years, he gave $16,400 for books and $11,000 for administration. In some years, Coolidge's gifts constituted more than twenty percent of new titles added and the dollar contribution was half the amount the university made available for book purchases. The total library budget in his last year as director was only $250,000 and the fund for books was $70,000 so his contributions were very important indeed.[32]

In addition, he contributed substantial funds for cataloguing. During his first five years as director, he supported reclassifying and recataloguing thousands of volumes and the introduction of standard Library of Congress cards. He paid the salary of the secretary of the Library Council and employed a number of graduate students to assist in library work, as cataloguers, curators of collections in which they were particularly interested, or purchasing agents abroad. His salary in 1919 was alloted to raising salaries of members of the library staff. His annual grants for administrative support in the 1920s were at least $3,000. While defending the Library budget request to the comptroller in 1922, he pointed out that he paid the salary of his secretary, although the university was responsible for his stationery, postage and library telephone bill.[33]

Modest and shy, Coolidge did not enjoy asking others to contribute to the library. Moreover, those who responded positively often later requested support for their favorite charities. Consequently, the secretary of the Library Council corresponded with graduates and friends of the university, while he approached only his family, former students, and close friends for purchasing special collections and for assisting generously in other ways. For example, his father not only gave $3,500 for the Ottoman field in 1899, but helped to buy the Riant collection the following year and contributed thereafter on the Arctic and Antarctic. Coolidge's brother Harold purchased extensively in the Asian field, and his uncle John Lowell Gardner not only contributed the salary of new faculty members but also gave substantial funds for library purchases. Another uncle granted $1,000 a year for books on Italy.

Even before 1910, Coolidge persuaded friends of Harvard to make annual gifts, from ten to several hundred dollars, for purchases in fields of interest to them, from Finnish folklore to medieval cities to the history of chemistry. Late in his career he succeeded in establishing a small informal organization of Friends of the Harvard University Library, which contributed to the collection and above all to understanding the role and needs of a library. The leading spirit of this group became Franklin Eddy Parker, Jr. of the class of 1918, who had traveled with Coolidge on trips between

1918 and 1922 and who made substantial gifts in eighteenth-century English literature.[34]

Above all, Coolidge encouraged many students to collect books; some later became great benefactors. John B. Stetson, Jr., a collector of Portuguese, Brazilian, and medieval French literature, as well as of Oscar Wilde, in 1926 gave Harvard 600 editions of works of Camoëns and in 1927 spent $75,000 for the Fernando Palha collection—10,000 volumes and 30,000 pamphlets on Portuguese history and literature. Bayard L. Kilgour, Jr., Harvard 1927, whom Coolidge and Blake had interested in Russia, began to collect books while a student of Coolidge, made his first of several trips to the Soviet Union while an undergraduate, and in 1956 presented Harvard a substantial collection of manuscripts and first editions of Russian poets and novelists. Robert Woods Bliss, Harvard 1900, a close friend of Coolidge as an undergraduate and throughout his diplomatic career, in 1913 established a chair in Latin American History and Economics and became interested in Byzantine history and culture, in large part because of Coolidge. The Dumbarton Oaks Library and Center for Byzantine Studies in Washington, which had 14,000 volumes when he and Mrs. Bliss presented it to Harvard in 1940, thus serves indirectly as a monument to Coolidge as well as to Mr. and Mrs. Bliss. James B. Munn of the Class of 1912 was secretary of the Library Council in 1916–1917, when he completed his Ph.D., and then served on the Visiting Committee. He and his father later became outstanding donors in the field of English literature of the sixteenth and seventeenth centuries. They presented books worth $60,000 in 1926 alone.[35]

Persuading students who became diplomats or businessmen to strengthen the library in fields of their interest and to help meet emergencies was another most successful tactic. Edwin V. Morgan, Harvard 1890, who completed his career in the Foreign Service by serving twenty years as American ambassador in Brazil, gave $2,500 each year for purchases on Latin America and also made other substantial gifts as opportunities and needs arose. Ellis L. Dresel, a classmate of Coolidge, assisted in building the collection on German drama, especially when in Germany as the United States High Commissioner after World War I. William B. Phillips, Harvard 1900, an important American diplomat, purchased books on the city of London. Another diplomat, Leland Harrison of the class of 1907, was interested in Bolivia and Colombia.[36]

August von Lengerke Meyer of the class of 1879 and a neighbor on Beacon Hill was also generous. When American ambassador in Rome from 1902 to 1905 he agreed that presenting books on modern Italian history would assist his mission. Later, he supplied Harvard with official Russian publications when he was ambassador in St. Petersburg. Julius

Klein, who wrote a thesis in Castilian history under Coolidge for his Ph.D. degree, was especially helpful when he was Assistant Secretary of Commerce and had many business friends in Latin America. J. P. Morgan, Jr., class of 1889, an overseer and a member of the Library Visiting Committee, gave $2,500 annually for books, especially in English poetry, and assisted when crises arose at the end of the budget year. Above all, he paid for the desks, chairs, and lamps for studies and carrels in Widener Library when that great building opened.[37]

Coolidge's influence extended throughout the American library world, not only because of his visible achievements at Harvard, but because he educated and excited Lichtenstein and other graduate students concerning the role of university libraries, their needs, and programs for enlarging and administering them. Many published useful bibliographies. Some became librarians. Frank Golder, who received his Ph.D. degree under Coolidge in 1909, became the first Director of the Hoover Institution. His purchases while in the Soviet Union in the 1920s created the foundations for the great Hoover collection on Russia. Lichtenstein served as Librarian at Northwestern University for more than ten years before becoming a successful Chicago banker. Jones, who was Coolidge's secretary in Paris in 1906–1907, worked in the library in 1909–1910, and obtained his Ph.D. degree in 1910, served as a professor of history and Director of the University Heights Library of New York University for thirty years with such distinction that Harvard awarded him the D. Litt in 1951. Most of those whose graduate work Coolidge directed, such as Robert J. Kerner at Berkeley and Albert H. Lybyer at Illinois, became strong supporters of the library in their institutions, while Lord was for sixteen years a trustee of the Boston Public Library.

Harvard's most obvious need when Coolidge became director of the library in 1910 was space. Within a year after his appointment, he outlined a long-term program and had architects prepare plans for a new building. Lowell was especially interested in constructing dormitories and laboratories, but Coolidge helped persuade him and the Corporation as well of the central role of the library. Lowell and Coolidge in January 1912 began to discuss ways of obtaining the several million dollars necessary for this building with wealthy Harvard alumni, such as J. P. Morgan, Jr. and Joseph Choate. The tragic death of Harry Elkins Widener, Harvard 1907, on the Titanic in April 1912 presented the opportunity they required.

An avid collector of rare books, in part because of Coolidge, Widener left his collection to the university as soon as it provided a proper place. Within a month of Widener's death and announcement of his will, Lowell and Coolidge had arranged that a copy of the library plans be in the hands of Widener's mother. Lowell, with assistance from Coolidge and Stetson, a close friend of Harry Elkins Widener and one of Mrs. Widener's closest advisers, persuaded her to provide a library building as a memorial, a generous and magnificent gift of about $4,000,000.[38]

Widener Library is one of the world's great library buildings. Designed by Horace Trumbauer, it dominates the Yard and remains the physical and spiritual center of the university. Its imposing entrance helps to provide both grandeur and serenity within the Yard, qualities the university needs because of the proximity of Harvard Square. The physical characteristics of the building itself are most impressive: Coolidge described them to the donor in 1920 as "unrivalled facilities in a magnificent setting." The reading rooms, the organization of the stacks, the 70 faculty studies, and the 300 carrels for graduate students were so arranged as to stimulate learning. They have made Widener a base and a center for research and instruction at Harvard and a model for other university library buildings in the United States.

In his years at Harvard, Coolidge "kept before the University and its friends a complete idea of the Library and its possibilities." Through his work with the faculty and the administration, particularly Lowell, he helped make the library an essential part of the university organization, an achievement many other institutions have not yet matched. He succeeded not only in creating a great library building, which is his "most conspicuous monument," but in providing a splendid organization, administration, and classification and cataloguing system. Widener became the center for research and study and an intellectual symbol of the university. The skill with which Coolidge anticipated future needs of the collection and the library as a whole created a magnet that has helped Harvard to attract and retain scholars and thereby to make it a great university. When Coolidge died, the Library was the fifth largest in the world and occupied "an assured position among the great libraries." The Harvard model of the federal library system and the quality of the entire library have inspired and perhaps even forced other American institutions to follow Harvard's splendid example.

ACKNOWLEDGEMENT

In preparing this article, I have benefited greatly from the opportunity for research and writing which the Netherlands Instituted For Advanced Study provided.

NOTES AND REFERENCES

1.   Harvard University Archives (hereafter cited as HUA), Coolidge letters to Charles H. Haskins, January 17, 1906, undated; Coolidge letters to Walter Lichtenstein, September 17, 1905; January 18, February 14, April 29, May 2, 1906; Roger B. Merriman, "Archibald

Cary Coolidge," *Harvard Graduates' Magazine*, XXXVI (1928), 553; William Bentinck-Smith, *Building a Great Library. The Coolidge Years at Harvard* (Cambridge, 1976), 22.

2. Council on Foreign Relations Archives (hereafter cited as CFRA), Tasker H. Bliss letter to Hamilton Fish Armstrong, January 28, 1928.

3. Archibald Cary Coolidge, "The Harvard College Library," *Harvard Graduates' Magazine*, XXIV (1915), 23; William S. Ferguson and others, "Archibald Cary Coolidge," *American Academy of Arts and Sciences Proceedings*, LXIV (1930), 514–516; Charles A. Wagner, *Harvard. Four Centuries and Freedoms* (New York, 1950), 178.

4. HUA, Coolidge, The Primacy of Harvard (Draft of 1915 Speech).

5. Coolidge, "The Harvard College Library," 30.

6. HUA, William Coolidge Lane, Diary, November 5, November 12, November 26, December 14, December 16, 1909; January 31, 1910; Laurence R. Veysey, *The Emergence of the American University* (Chicago, 1965), 178; Bentinck-Smith, *Building a Great Library*, 10.

7. HUA, Coolidge, Survey of the Library, 1910; Coolidge letter to Lichtenstein, January 31, 1910; Coolidge, "Crying Needs of the Library," *Harvard Graduates' Magazine*, XIX (1911), 410–411; Coolidge, "The Harvard College Library," 26–28; Harvard University. Committee Appointed to Study the Future Needs of the College Library, *Report Presented March 31, 1902* (Cambridge, 1902), 3–10, 20–21; *Harvard University Library, 1636–1968* (Cambridge, 1969), 13–14; William Coolidge Lane, "The Harvard College Library," in Samuel Eliot Morison (editor), *The Development of Harvard University since the Inauguration of President Eliot, 1869–1929* (Cambridge, 1930), 629; Bentinck-Smith, *Building a Great Library*, 23–27, 170.

8. HUA, Coolidge to Lichtenstein, June 3, July 9, July 16, July 26, August 4, 1912; Ernest Cushing Richardson letter to William Coolidge Lane, April 16, 1928; Harvard University. Medical School. Library Committee Minute, 1928; Keyes D. Metcalf, *Report on the Harvard University Library. A Study of Present and Prospective Problems* (Cambridge, 1955), 49; Bentinck-Smith, *Building a Great Library*, 148–151.

9. HUA, Coolidge letter to William R. Castle, Jr., December 18, 1912; Thomas Franklin Currier, "A Sheaf of Memories from the Cataloguers," *Harvard Library Notes*, Number 20, April, 1928, 167–168; George Parker Winship, "Archibald Cary Coolidge," *Harvard Library Notes*, Number 20, 1928, 157; Bentinck-Smith, *Building a Great Library*, 34.

10. Coolidge, "The Objects of Cataloging," *Library Journal*, XLVI (1921), 735–739; Currier, "A Sheaf of Memories," 107.

11. HUA, Coolidge letters to Lichtenstein, January 2, February 1, 1911; Coolidge letter to Thomas F. Currier, December 22, 1927; Coolidge, "The Objects of Cataloging," 735–737; Lane, "The Harvard College Library," 618, 621; Bentinck-Smith, *Building a Great Library*, 38–44.

12. HUA, Coolidge letter to Mrs. Hamilton Rice, August 19, 1920; Paul Buck, *Libraries and Universities. Addresses and Reports* (Cambridge, 1964), 74.

13. Coolidge, "Crying Needs of the Library," 411; Currier, "A Sheaf of Memories," 132; Bentinck-Smith, *Building a Great Library*, 104–105.

14. HUA, Ernest Cushing Richardson letter to Lane, April 16, 1928; Coolidge letter to Lichtenstein, March 13, 1913; CFRA, Coolidge letter to Hamilton Fish Armstrong, February 16, 1925; *Harvard Library Notes*, Number 20, April, 1928, 154–155; Currier, "A Sheaf of Memories," 132.

15. "Resources of American Libraries," *Annual Report of the American Historical Association for the Year 1922* (Washington, 1926), I, 243–245; Winifred Gregory (editor), *Union List of Serials in Libraries of the United States and Canada* (New York, 1927), preface.

16. Lucius M. Beebe, *Boston and the Boston Legend* (New York, 1935), 205.

17. Melville J. Ruggles, "Eastern European Publications in American Libraries," in Howard W. Winger (editor), *Iron Curtains and Scholarship. The Exchange of Knowledge in a Divided World* (Chicago, 1958), 113–114; Paul L. Horecky, "The Slavic and East European Resources and Facilities of the Library of Congress," *Slavic Review*, XXIII (1964), 309–312; Frank Golder, *Russian Expansion on the Pacific, 1641–1850* (Cleveland, 1914), 340.

18. Phyllis Dain, *The New York Public Library. A History of Its Founding and Early Years* (New York, 1972), 114–119; Avrahm Yarmolinsky, "The Slavonic Division, Recent Growth," *Bulletin of the New York Public Library*, XXX (1926), 71–77; Ruggles, "Eastern European Publications," 112; Interview with Avrahm Yarmolinsky, January 6, 1973.

19. Herbert Hoover, *An American Epic* (Chicago, 1959–1964), I, 184–185, 327–328; III, 454–455; *Hoover Institution on War, Revolution and Peace* (Stanford, 1963), 1–3; Harold H. Fisher, *The Famine in Soviet Russia, 1919–1923. The Operations of the American Relief Administration* (New York, 1927), 466, 563; Charles B. Burdick, *Ralph Lutz and the Hoover Institution* (Stanford, 1973), 8–9, 23–32, 38, 45, 47, 80–83; Paul Miliukov, *Political Memoirs*. Edited by Arthur P. Mendel. Translated by Carl Goldberg (Ann Arbor, 1967), 198; *American Historical Review*, XXVI (1921), 622.

20. HUA, Lane, Diary, April 4, April 7, May 17, November 15, 1898; Otto Harrassowitz Buchhandlung und Antiquariat in Leipzig, *Antiquarischer Catalog 202. Slavica* (Leipzig, 1895); Dmitry Cizevsky, "The Slovak Collection of the Harvard College Library," *Harvard Library Bulletin*, 7 (1953), 299–311; Ruggles, "Eastern European Publications," 112; Bentinck-Smith, *Building a Great Library*, 11.

21. HUA, Coolidge letters to his father, December 4, 1921, January 4, 1922; Coolidge letters to Frank Golder, October 2, 1922; May 1, 1923; Coolidge letters to Walter R. Batsell, February 8, 1924; February 14, 1925; Batsell letters to Coolidge, January 20, March 29, September 2, 1925; Coolidge letters to Robert J. Kerner, October 15, 1912; July 23, 1914; October 7, 1924; Michael Rostovtsev letter to Coolidge, January 24, 1927; Coolidge letter to Rostovtsev, January 25, 1927; "The Russian Books," *Harvard Library Notes*, November 9, 1922, 203–209; Wilbur H. Siebert, "Collections of Materials in English and European History and Subsidiary Fields in the Libraries of the United States," American Historical Association *Annual Report, 1904* (Washington, D.C., 1905), 693–694; Charles R. Gredler, "The Slavic Collection at Harvard," *Harvard Library Bulletin*, XVII (1969), 431; Bentinck-Smith, *Building a Great Library*, 126–128, 156, 167.

22. HUA, Lane, Diary, April 5, April 10, September 29, October 2–6, 1899; Count Paul de Riant, *Catalogue de la bibliothèque de feu M. le comte Riant* (Paris, 1896–1899), II, page opposite title page; Harold Jefferson Coolidge and Robert H. Lord, *Archibald Cary Coolidge. Life and Letters* (Boston, 1932), 45–47; Bentinck-Smith, *Building a Great Library*, 13.

23. HUA, Lane, Diary, April 5, April 10, September 29, October 2–6, 1899; Albert H. Lybyer, *The Government of the Ottoman Empire in the Time of Suleiman the Magnificent* (Cambridge, 1913), 308; Stanford Shaw, *The Harvard College Library Collection of Books on Ottoman History and Literature* (Cambridge, 1959; Typescript), preface; Labib Yamak, "Introduction. The Middle Eastern Collections of the Harvard Library," in Harvard University Library, *Catalogue of Arabic, Persian, and Ottoman Turkish Books* (Cambridge, 1968), I, vii–ix; Alfred Claghorn Potter, *The Library of Harvard University* (Cambridge, 1934), Fourth edition, 66, 118; Winship, "Coolidge," 158–159.

24. HUA, Lane, Diary, February 20, 1905; Papers and other Documents concerning Prof. Coolidge's Gift of the Hohenzollern Collection to the Harvard College Library and the Opening of the Germanic Museum; Harvard University Library. Routine records. Duplicates and Exchanges, "Katalog der bibliothek des verstorbenen Universität professors Konrad von Maurer;" Coolidge letter to Edwin V. Morgan, November 14, 1903; Coolidge letters to Lichtenstein, June 9, June 12, 1909; October 1, 1910; Lichtenstein letters to

Coolidge, July 15, July 21, August 6, September 18, September 30, November 8, November 30, 1905; March 10, 1906; Kuno Francke letters to Coolidge, October 26, October 30, December 7, 1903; Walter R. Batsell letters to Coolidge, October 6, November 22, 1924; Coolidge letter to Batsell, December 8, 1924; Potter, *The Library*, 88–90, 125; Winship, "Coolidge," 160; Washington *Times*, November 19, 1903; Boston *Transcript*, November 10–11, 1903; *American Historical Review*, XI (1905) 213–214.

25. HUA, Coolidge letter to Charles H. Haskins, January 17, 1906; Coolidge letters to Lichtenstein, March 28, 1908; November 28, 1910; Lichtenstein letters to Coolidge, August 27, 1907; March 28, 1908; August 26, 1910; Harvard University Library. Chronological Miscellany, W. Lichtenstein Report on Trip to Europe, 1905–1906; Report of W. Lichtenstein on European History Department, 1906–1907; Lichtenstein, Report on the Hohenzollern Collection of German History, October 1903–May 1905; Lichtenstein, Hohenzollern Collection, 1904–1914; Lichtenstein, Purchases on South American Trips, 1914; Lichtenstein, Report to the President of Northwestern University on the Results of a Trip to South America (Evanston, 1915); Lichtenstein, Statement about his career and especially his relations with A. C. Coolidge and his contribution to the Harvard Library, 27 June 1956, especially 1–4.

26. HUA, Coolidge letter to Haskins, January 17, 1906; Bentinck-Smith, *Building a Great Library*, 133–135, 141.

27. HUA, Coolidge letter to Lane, February 8, 1907; Coolidge letter to Haskins, June 6, 1922; Philip M. Hamer (editor), *A Guide to Archives and Manuscripts in the United States* (New Haven, 1961), 252–254; Potter, *The Library*, 86; Bentinck-Smith, *Building a Great Library*, 18–19.

28. National Archives, Department of State Decimal File, 1910–1929, Coolidge letter to William B. Castle, Jr., February 19, 1924; HUA, Coolidge letter to Morgan, January 16, 1912; Bentinck-Smith, *Building a Great Library*, 57–58, 142–143.

29. HUA, Coolidge letters to Lichtenstein, February 15, 1909; July 7, August 11, October 16, October 17, October 23, October 25, October 30, 1911; January 23, June 3, June 12, 1912; March 26, March 29, April 7, April 29, 1913; Lichtenstein letters to Coolidge, March 29, March 25, April 29, 1913; Coolidge letters to Morgan, September 27, 1910; July 13, 1912; December 25, 1914; April 27, 1916; Coolidge letters to Hiram Bingham, March 29, April 26, May 2, 1913; Bingham letters to Coolidge, May 1, May 5, 1913; November 8, November 15, 1915; Lichtenstein letter to Bingham, May 2, 1913; Potter, *The Library*, 105, 172; Bentinck-Smith, *Building a Great Library*, 22, 114; *American Historical Review*, XV (1910), 472. The correspondence among Bingham, Coolidge, and Lichtenstein from April through June 1913 is voluminous.

30. HUA, Coolidge letter to W. S. Howe, September 18, 1925; Siebert, "Collections of Materials," 622, 680; Coolidge and Lord, *Coolidge*, 47. Almost fifty years later, another member of the clan, Thomas Jefferson Coolidge, IV, Harvard 1954, headed a $20,000,000 drive to strengthen the university's Asian collection and program, demonstrating the continued interest of the family in the library's resources on Asia. At that time, the Harvard-Yenching Institute library contained more than 500,000 volumes. (Paula Cronin, "East Asian Studies at Harvard. A Scholarly Bridge between two Worlds," *Harvard Today*, Spring, 1976, 7–9, 13).

31. Ray Billington (editor), *Dear Lady. The Letters of Frederick Jackson Turner to Alice Forbes Perkins Hooper, 1910–1932* (San Marino, California, 1970), 15–16, 20, 25–26, 53–69, 103, 118, 156–163, 210, 224, 304–305, 396, 423–424; Bentinck-Smith, *Building a Great Library*, 115–120.

32. Harvard University Library total operating expenditures in 1949 were $1,700,000, in 1969 more than $9,000,000, and in 1979, $19,000,000.

33. HUA, Lane, Diary, October 15, 1900; January 3, January 13, February 13, 1905;

November 10, 1908; March 24, May 24, July 30, 1909; October 15, 1910; Coolidge letter to Lichtenstein, July 11, 1911; *The Letters of William Roscoe Thayer*. Edited by Charles Downer Hazen (Boston, 1926), 140–141; Coolidge and Lord, *Coolidge*, 87; Bentinck-Smith, *Building a Great Library*, 108–109, 141–142, 157, 168–169, 204.

34. Winship, "Coolidge," 162–164, 172–176; Bentinck-Smith, *Building a Great Library*, 107–108, 120–122, 134, 177–180.

35. HUA, Coolidge letters to Morgan, February 10, 1901; December 25, 1914; April 27, 1916; Coolidge letters to Lichtenstein, May 15, August 10, 1914; Coolidge letters to J. P. Morgan, Jr., September 17, September 25, 1915; Coolidge letters to Robert Woods Bliss, October 23, 1920; October 27, 1922; September 16, 1924; Bliss letter to Coolidge, October 29, 1920; Coolidge letters to Castle, November 24, 1925; March 27; June 25, 1926; Charles L. Chandler letter to Harold Jefferson Coolidge, November 23, 1932; CFRA, Coolidge letters to Hamilton Fish Armstrong, October 10, 1922; May 6, 1927; Harvard University Library. *The Kilgour Collection of Russian Literature, 1750–1920* (Cambridge, 1959), preface, 201; Gredler, "The Slavic Collection," 429–430; Winship, "Coolidge," 161; Bentinck-Smith, *Building a Great Library*, 105, 129–133, 139–140.

36. HUA, Lane, Diary, February 11, 1907; Coolidge letters to Lichtenstein, November 19, 1905; January 17, 1912; Lichtenstein letters to Coolidge, November 7, 1913; September 10, 1914; Ellis Dresel letters to Coolidge, December 12, 1919; October 2, 1920; April 12, 1921; Coolidge letter to Dresel, January 12, 1921; W. Cameron Forbes letter to Coolidge, March 16, 1922; John A. Gade, *All My Born Days* (New York, 1942), 297–298; Morison, *The Development of Harvard University*, 84–85.

37. HUA, Coolidge letter to Edwin V. Morgan, December 26, 1902; Coolidge letters to Kerner, July 13, July 23, 1914; Julius Klein letter to Coolidge, January 5, 1924; Mark A. D. Howe, *George von Lengerke Meyer: His Life and Public Services* (New York, 1920), 5–6.

38. HUA, Coolidge letter to Edwin V. Morgan, August 14, 1912; Coolidge letters to Lichtenstein, May 24, June 3, July 16, 1912; Coolidge letter to Mrs. Hamilton Rice, August 19, 1920; Yeomans, *Lowell*, 238–240; Bentinck-Smith, *Building a Great Library* 50–77.

LIBRARY AUTOMATION:
BUILDING AND EQUIPMENT
CONSIDERATIONS IN
IMPLEMENTING
COMPUTER TECHNOLOGY

Edwin B. Brownrigg

Like many of the technological accomplishments of this century such as the airplane, the automobile, and mass communication media, the general application and use of the computer is easily grasped. Its specific application and use, particularly in libraries, however, is not so easily grasped. To be sure, computers enjoy a demonstrable role in library service. On-line reference and on-line cataloging services are evidence of this role.

But what about installing not just time-sharing computer terminals but rather computers themselves as an integral part of a library operation? A

Advances in Library Administration and Organization, volume 1, pages 43–53
Copyright © 1982 by JAI PRESS INC.
All rights of reproduction in any form reserved.
ISBN: 0-89232-213-6

discussion of this proposition among a group of ten library administrators would probably produce varying reactions, such as:

1. Time sharing on someone else's computer is the only solution for my library.
2. My library doesn't have the resources to install computers larger than micro processors.
3. Turnkey computer systems are OK for my library, because the vendor absorbs the site preparation and installation headaches.
4. Because my library requires an integrated public and technical processing system, which to be cost effective must be computer-based, computer center site preparation and installation management are part of my library plan.

Library administrators and managers in groups 2, 3, and 4, in ascending order of benefit, will be interested in the following discussion.

I. *SCHEDULING*
    In order to install any computer, there must be a plan. For there to be a plan, there must be a schedule. If we can assume as a working hypothesis that the requisition and purchase of the computer is an accomplished fact, then we must concern ourselves with the following aspects of a schedule.

A. *Twelve Months Prior to Installation*
    1. *Complete inventory* of each and every discrete piece of hardware to be installed including:
        • brand name
        • model number
        • features and options
    2. Location of each item in above
    3. Meetings with vendor and affected management staff to review installation
    4. Determination of special requirements as a result of (3) above
    5. Determination of availability and delivery of:
        • Power   • Security device
        • Air conditioning   • Other (nonstatic rugs, etc.)
        • Cable

B. *Six Months*
    Review of A above for Go/No-go decision

C. *Four Months*
   1. Commit to installation configuration
   2. Adjust cabling according to C-1

D. *Two Weeks*
   1. Lay cables
   2. Deliver field engineering furniture

E. *One Week*
   1. Air conditioning fully operational
   2. Electrical power fully operational
   3. All building renovations completed
   4. All building security arrangements made for delivery:
      - adequate passageway
      - Short-term receiving environment

II. *PHYSICAL CONSIDERATIONS*
   The schedule discussed above could easily be described in a PERT chart. Each of the lines and their respective items could be represented in the discussion below:

A. *Building Requirements*
   1. Availability and location of adequate electrical power and backup:
      - power regulation
      - orderly shut-down back-up supply
   2. Space for air conditioning units and conduction
   3. Finished floor-to-ceiling walls:
      - security
      - air conditioning insulation
   4. Work flow to other areas
   5. Floor loading capacity
   6. Fire safety and fire prevention
   7. Electromagnetic interference

B. *The System Layout*
   The installation manager should be prepared to trade off operational requirements and conveniences with physical restrictions on the co-location of equipment. For example, individual system components are often required to be within constrained proximity to each other on account of cable lengths; spacing between components is compactable only to the limit of

space taken up by opening chassis doors; and, peripheral equipment like disk drives need to be geographically aligned and sequenced with respect to their governing communications channels.

C. *Floor Construction*

Floor loading applies only to large computer center installations, and the library installing such a system should work closely with its vendor to conform to vendor specifications.

Whether or not the vendor requires it, the library will be well advised to plan for a raised floor for the installation of a minicomputer or larger machine in order to accomplish the following objectives:

1. Allow for future layout change with minimum reconstruction cost
2. Protect cables and receptacles
3. Permit the space between the two floors to supply air for equipment and personnel

Raised floors can be made of steel, aluminum, or fire-resistant wood cut into tiles which fit together over a subframe. Wooden floors avoid the need for floor covering which must be used with metal floors in order to insulate staff from electrical safety hazard. If floor coverings are used they should be certified as antistatic.

Floors must be cleaned thoroughly and regularly in order to protect the machine from harmful dust and grease. Vacuum cleaner nozzles should be nonconductive, and scrubbing brushes should be of nonmetallic brush only.

D. *Furniture*

Furniture should be certified as nonstatic. The chairs' points of contact with the floor should measure ohms at nine orders of magnitude less than any metal in the chair. Casters and ball bearings should be lubricated with graphite, not grease.

E. *Acoustical Treatment of Computer Room*

Acoustical treatment contributes to a more comfortable and therefore more efficient operation. Noise levels can be minimized by placing noisy equipment in relatively empty space and away from operators. Air conditioning blowers should not be overlooked as sources of noise. Sound-absorptive ceilings and walls are essential to dampen noise between the computer room and the surrounding offices.

F. *Electromagnetic Compatibility*

It is not recommended that a computer be located in proximity to radio frequency generating equipment such as radio transmitters, two-way radio stations, radar, induction heaters, arc welders, and so forth. Reciprocally, computer programs randomly cause computer circuitry to resonate at radio frequencies that can interfere with radio and television receivers.

G. *Lighting*

Direct sunlight should be avoided, because it causes heat and because lower levels of ambient illumination are required to observe consoles and lamps. A minimum illumination of 50–75 foot candles (540–800 lumens)/square meter measured 30 inches (76 cm) above the floor should be maintained. Lighting should be sectionally controlled and circuited completely independently from computer equipment.

H. *Air Conditioning*

It is highly unlikely that libraries will install computer equipment that requires direct water cooling. Rather, it will be internally cooled by air circulated by blowers within individual units.

The quantity of conditioned air is a function of the following:

- Machine heat dissipation
- Personnel
- Latent load
- Fresh air introduction
- Infiltration of heat through outer walls
- Floors
- Door openings
- Ceiling
- Partitions
- Glass wall areas
- Possible reheat

1. *Temperature, Humidity, and Operating Limits*

Temperature and humidity should be maintained at 75 degrees Fahrenheit (24°C) and 50% relative humidity. The median between most machine operating temperature limits is 75°F.

	Machine Operating	Machine Non-Operating	Design Criteria
Temperature	60° to 90°F	50° to 110°F	75°F
	16° to 32°C	10° to 43°C	24°C
Relative Humidity	20% to 80%	8% to 80%	5%
Max Wet Bulb	78°F (26°C)	80°F (27°C)	—

Air conditioning control instruments that respond to ±2°F (1±1°C) and ±5% relative humidity should be installed.

In many geographical areas, it is necessary to add moisture to the machine room in order to meet design criteria. This may be accomplished through one of the following methods:

- steam grid or jets
- steam cup
- water atomizers

If the natural water supply is high in mineral content, it should be treated so as to avoid contamination of the air. In areas where outside temperatures drop considerably below freezing, the outside walls of the building should be water-proofed or vapor-sealed, or structural damage will occur in the outside wall.

2. *Air Filtration*

Machine room air should be filtered according to vendor specifications. If a mechanical air filter is used, a rating of a minimum of 20% efficiency by Bureau of Standards discoloration test using atmospheric dust is recommended. If an electrostatic plate filter is used, a rating of a minimum of 85 to 90% efficiency is recommended. Electrostatic filters have the disadvantage when not maintained of passing charged particles into the machine room which cause dust to accumulate rapidly on all surfaces, thus defeating the purpose of air filtration.

3. *Temperature and Humidity Recording Instruments*

These instruments should be installed in order to keep a record of temperature and humidity that can be used to:

1. Assure that the air conditioning and humidifier equipment is functioning normally
2. Signal the necessity for a dry-out period
3. Determine if the environment meets vendor specifications

Direct reading instruments with seven-day charts are standard in most computer installations.

III. *POWER REQUIREMENTS*

Power requirements vary depending on the type of computer equipment involved. Requirements for alternating power supplied by the local power company are typically 115 or 208 volts, one or three phase at 60 cycles. Total system power can be estimated by summing the KVA ratings of each individual device.

A. *Voltage Limits*

The line-to-line, steady-state voltage must be maintained within plus 10% or minus 8% of the normal rated voltage, measured at the receptacle when the unit is operating.

A transient voltage condition must not exceed plus 15% or minus 18% of normal and must return to within a steady-state tolerance of plus 10% or minus 8% of the normal rated voltage within 30 cycles. Where brownouts are possible, voltage monitoring and alarm equipment should be installed. Any computer vendor not supplying, or at least requiring power regulating equipment should be suspect.

B. *Frequency Limits*

Generally ± ½ Hz is the limit of toleration.

C. *Line-to-Line Imbalance*

In three-phase systems, voltage should not differ by more than 25% from the arithmetic average of the three voltages.

IV. *POWER DISTRIBUTION SYSTEM*

A. *Primary Computer Power Service*

For maximum efficiency, the computer power panel should connect to feeders that serve no other loads.

B. *Branch Circuits*

The computer branch circuit panel should be in an unobstructed, well-lighted area in the computer room.

The individual branch circuits should be protected by suitable circuit breakers.

Grounding wires should be insulated and equal in size to the phase conductors.

Branch circuits should terminate under the raised floor as close as possible to the machine they supply. They should run within metallic conduit.

C. *Emergency and Unit Emergency Power-Off Controls*

Each individual component should have its own unit emergency power-off control. In addition, controls should be provided for disconnecting the main service wiring supplying all of the computer equipment. These controls should be convenient to the operator and next to main exit doors.

D. *Lightning Protection*

Lightning is disastrous for computers. Lightning protection should be installed on the secondary power source when:

1. The primary power is supplied by an overhead service
2. The utility company installs lightning protectors on the primary power source
3. The area is subject to electrical storms or equivalent types of power surges

Vendors are usually uncooperative in specifying lightning protection.

E. *Convenience Outlets*

A suitable number of convenience outlets should be installed in the computer room and customer engineering room for use by building maintenance personnel, porter service, customer engineers, and so forth. These must be circuited independently from computer branch circuits.

V. *SAFETY AND FIRE PRECAUTIONS*

A. *Computer Location*

The computer should be in a noncombustible or fire-resistant building or room. Adjacent rooms should not contain hazardous materials like volatile chemicals.

B. *Good Fire Prevention Considerations*

1. Walls enclosing the computer area should extend from the structural floor to the structural ceiling and be rated at a mimimum of one-hour fire resistance.
2. Where a false (or hung) ceiling is to be added, it should be constructed of noncombustible or fire-resistant material.
3. A raised floor should also be constructed of fire-retardant or noncombustible materials.
4. If a fire occurs and water is used to extinguish it, then
   a. The ceiling should be water tight;
   b. Run-off drainage should be built into the floor.

C. *Choices of Fire Prevention Equipment*

An early warning detection system should be installed to protect the staff, the computer and the storage media. Readily accessible portable fire extinguishers should be provided as the initial line of defense and, as a secondary extinguishing agent, a standpipe or hose unit should be available. Automatic fire extinguishing equipment is appropriate for large machine rooms. Carbon dioxide is the least desirable of such systems because of its toxicity. A water sprinkler system is also undesirable because of its harmful effect on electronic equipment. Holon 1301 is the most highly recommended room-flooding system because it is effective as a fire extinguishing agent and is harmless to people and equipment.

VI. *SECURITY ANALYSIS*

By adhering to the foregoing prescriptions, the computer center manager can establish a highly reliable environment in which to install and run a computer. At this point, it is important to protect this investment through the processes of security analysis and disaster planning.

In the context of computers, the word "security" is generally associated with "invasion of privacy." But in terms of the computer center installation itself, it more narrowly refers to the uninterrupted accomplishment of the center's mission through "fail-safe" precautions. To develop a physical security program, the following procedures are appropriate:

1. Analyze risk as the basis for the development of a security policy.
2. Select and implement appropriate security measures to reduce exposure to losses.
3. Develop contingency plans for backup operation, disaster recovery, and emergencies.
4. Train personnel.
5. Plan and conduct continued tests and audits, and adjust security measures and contingency plans as needed.

A. *What are the most prevalent threats to a computer center?*

1. Unauthorized access
2. Hardware failure
3. Failure of supporting utilities
4. Natural disasters

5. Nonavailability of key personnel
6. Neighboring hazards
7. Telecommunications interruptions

Risk analysis should include for each of these threats or catastrophes:

1. Probability of occurrence
2. Impact on the information system
3. Impact on the organization
4. The cost of protecting against threats

The analyst should devise the set of curves showing how the probability of system failure varies with the amount spent on protection for various impact cost thresholds. Top management must draw the line between expenses involved in calculating risks and protecting against them:

Risks

1. Physical destruction or theft of tangible assets
2. Loss of data or program files
3. Theft of information
4. Delayed processing

Threats from Natural Disasters

1. Fire
2. Flood
3. Earthquake
4. Windstorm
5. Power failure
6. Air conditioning failure
7. Communications failures
8. Hardware failure
9. Intruders, vandals
10. Internal theft or misuse
11. Invasion of privacy

Selecting remedial measures for each of these situations is a subject in itself, but common to all of them are four elements.

1. Planning
2. Prevention
3. Early detection
4. Trained response

Planning must involve top management and prevention must be a continually executed part of the plan. Prevention includes:

1. Adherence to installation standards and codes
2. Cyclical data set backup
3. Hardware preventive maintenance

Probably the most weighty decision in disaster planning is how to allocate costs for recovery from a complete disaster. Assuming that all data sets are backed-up, then what is it worth to the organization to:

1. Maintain site and hardware backup?
2. Install switchable telecommunication circuits?

These are rough questions, but are best answered and dealt with cooperatively. It is common for many data processing organizations in a given geographical area with common processing styles to pool resources and share costs for full-scale disaster contingency plans.

Computer centers should be planned for disaster. A well-planned center should incorporate these five lessons:

1. One of Murphy's Laws: Prepare for the worst because it will happen.
2. Top management *and* users must be involved in key design decisions.
3. It is unwise to spend all resources to protect against catastrophes and leave nothing for planning and preparing for their occurrence.
4. Don't go it alone.
5. Be practical.

BIBLIOGRAPHY

"Checklist for Data Center Facilities. Part 1: Site Requirements and Selection." In: Auerbach Publishers Inc. *Data Center Operations.* 26-01-01 Management of the Facility. 1977.

Gilchrist, Bruce. "Coping with Catastrophe: Implications to Information System Design." *Journal of the American Society for Information Science.* November 1978. pp. 271–277.

International Business Machines Corporation. *IBM System/370 Installation Manual-Physical Planning.* 6th ed. 1977. GC22-7004-5.

International Business Machines Corporation. Data Processing Division. *Organizing the Data Processing Activity.* 3rd. ed. 1973. GC20-1622-2.

National Fire Protection Agency. *Standards for the Protection of Electronic Computer/ Data Processing Equipment, No. 75.* 1976.

U.S. Department of Commerce. National Bureau of Standards. *Guidelines for Automatic Data Processing, Physical Security and Risk Management.* Publication no. 31. June 1974. p. 91.

THE MICROFORMS FACILITY
AT THE GOLDA MEIR LIBRARY
OF THE UNIVERSITY OF
WISCONSIN-MILWAUKEE

William C. Roselle

The design of the present microforms facility at the Golda Meir Library of the University of Wisconsin-Milwaukee began in 1971 as part of the construction planning for the second stage of the library's physical facility. In approaching the design of this microforms facility, my colleagues and I were presented with a dual problem: to provide for storage, retrieval, and patron access and acceptance factors of microforms while at the same time adapting an existing facility to those unique requirements.

In sharing our experiences in developing what has proven over the past decade to be a reasonably successful microforms facility, I intend to: (1) identify those principal considerations that we found of greatest im-

Advances in Library Administration and Organization, volume 1, pages 55–68
Copyright © 1982 by JAI PRESS INC.
All rights of reproduction in any form reserved.
ISBN: 0-89232-213-6

portance in the initial design and of significant long-term value to the facility's ability to serve readers; (2) share information on problems that we encountered; (3) call attention through the bibliography to writings that we found useful in 1971 during facility design as well as other important contributions to the literature that have appeared during the intervening years; (4) provide assistance to colleagues who may have opportunity to remodel or expand existing microforms facilities; and (5) invite suggestions, comments, and the sharing of similar experiences from readers of this volume. The last is this essay's *raison d'être*.

In approaching our design of the microforms facility at UWM, we were forced to recognize two unfortunate but frequently encountered inconsistencies in academic librarianship. Librarians have expended vast amounts of money for the acquisition of microform collections and equipment and far larger sums for the construction of library buildings, but our profession often leaves users with the impression that we are either unable or unwilling to provide comfortable and successful microform reading rooms. In too many instances, such positive and essential considerations as efficiency in space use and assignment, esthetics (in furnishings, decor, and arrangement), and layouts conducive to effective user services and efficient microforms storage are woefully lacking. Secondly, our literature contains a richness of information on virtually all elements of microforms librarianship, but, until quite recently, precious little stood on the shelves to guide the practicing librarian who was faced with an assignment to design a microforms room, either as part of a new contruction project or for inclusion in renovated quarters in an existing facility.

A large portion of the culpability for shortcomings in the provision of microform facilities must be assumed by librarianship, but our profession is not solely at fault. In many instances, hard-pressed librarians and their much-maligned library administrators did everything humanly possible to determine and to meet the facilities requirements of microform storage and access. Failure to achieve totally satisfactory results can, in this author's opinion, be only infrequently, if ever, attributed to librarians' ignorance of or lack of concern for and attention to the specifics of owning and servicing microforms. A crushing array of variables can intervene and are doubtless more to be blamed than is Charles T. Meadow's painful but sometimes accurate observation concerning the "lack of interest by many library administrators, resulting in poor physical and psychological conditions for use of microfilms in libraries."

Frequently, there is no member of the library's professional staff who has the title or assignment of microforms librarian. Many times, there is no professional staff committee which has microforms policies and practices within its purview. Architects and facilities planners fail to identify, or else ignore entirely, the unique requirements of microforms.

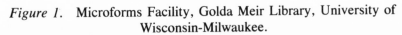

Figure 1. Microforms Facility, Golda Meir Library, University of
Wisconsin-Milwaukee.

Institutions have been unable or unwilling to provide the funding necessary to ensure satisfactory or even adequate microform reading rooms.
The growth of microform collections and requisite user services has out-
stripped facilities planning and space assignment. Microform equipment
manufacturers have provided little in the way of consulting assistance,
and limited information on microforms facilities design has been available
at professional meetings. In many instances, archaic library buildings
have imposed inescapable strictures of brick and mortar. And, finally,
limited opportunity, funding, or initiative have been available to support
research that might result in the kinds of guidance needed in the area of
microforms facility design.

The Golda Meir Library at the University of Wisconsin-Milwaukee
(UWM) provides centralized library collections and services in support
of the instructional, research, and service programs of one of the two
doctoral degree-granting institutions in the twenty-seven-campus University of Wisconsin System. UWM offers sixty-nine baccalaureate majors,
forty-two master's degrees, and fifteen doctoral programs through its
twelve schools and colleges. Enrollment in the first semester of the 1980–
81 academic year was 25,933.

UWM was founded in 1956 as the result of an educational merger
approved by the Wisconsin Legislature. UWM has consistently empha-

sized the development of its library holdings, and the collections have grown from approximately 114,000 volumes in 1956 to more than 2.6 million items in 1981. The largest and most significant single acquisition was the 1978 transfer of the 600,000 items in the American Geographical Society Collection from New York City to UWM. The June 30, 1980 collection totals, not including the geographical holdings, are: 1,174,187 volumes; 841,866 microforms; 3,147 audiovisual items; and 1,412 records and tapes.

The first stage of the library was opened in February, 1967. It provided 151,475 gross square feet at a construction cost of $3.6 million. The library's second stage was opened in May, 1974. It provides 114,734 gross square feet and was completed at a cost of $4.3 million. Construction of the second stage included courtyard columns for support of the third and final stage of the library's facility. As we open the 1981 calendar, no state funding or construction timetable has been established for the needed third stage of the facility, but that proposed construction retains its high priority, established in 1976, among UWM's facilities needs.

In 1971, our design of a microforms facility was complicated by several absolutes: (1) the microforms facility would occupy existing space in a facility that would be remodeled as part of the construction project of a building addition; (2) the space selected for the microforms facility already housed microforms, an instructional materials center, and all of the music collection; (3) minimal funding was available for renovation or for equipment purchase; (4) the campus facilities committee and the project architect gave the librarian *carte blanche* to research, develop, design, and implement plans for the microforms facility; and (5) success or failure would be determined by the librarian. (I am reminded here of General Rommel's observation that victory can claim many fathers, but defeat is always an orphan.)

Our first steps were to search the literature, make several site visits, talk to selected microforms librarians, examine our microforms collection and service to be certain that we knew what we were working with, attempt to assess the state of the art and (a virtual impossibility) portend future technological advances, determine where we wanted our microforms unit to go (or where we wished to take it—in concept, not physically), establish equipment needs (readers, printers, shelving, cabinets, etc.), and, only after the aforementioned had been thoroughly addressed, attempt to get all this in place on the architect's working drawings.

Our initial decision, the location of the microforms room within the library facility, essentially was not open for debate for it had been made for us by the physical aspects of the building's first stage construction and by the project's budget. We were committed to an L-shaped area of approximately 4,000 square feet on the lower level of the building's first

Figure 2. Microforms Service Desk and Centralized Storage of Microforms, Golda Meir Library, University of Wisconsin-Milwaukee.

stage. In accepting this space for microforms, it was necessary for us to relocate the instructional materials collection and the music collection to quarters in the building's new, second phase. Those two collections had, of necessity, been sharing crowded quarters with microforms for a number of years, and staff were eager for new space.

It was also decided that we would centralize all microforms in a single location. That microforms centralization was to include all collections, all equipment, and all services. The only exception was the transfer of the ERIC microfiche to the building's planned second stage along with the instructional materials collection. That was, in 1971, a troublesome consideration for it ran counter to our philosophy of microforms centralization, but it has since proven to be a sound decision for it placed the ERIC microfiche in the department frequently used by students and faculty from the School of Education.

Centralization of microforms was reinforced by campus philosophy and by the building's physical arrangements. During the early 1970s, UWM's campus administration and faculty committees were assessing the relative merits of decentralized versus centralized university library collections and services. A faculty referendum overwhelmingly supported administration's plans for library centralization, and all collections and services have been maintained under one roof since 1974. Resource centers of a specialized nature exist in several Schools or Colleges at UWM, but those are not supported by the library's budget or staffing allocations. Physical arrangements strengthening a decision in favor of the use of this L-shaped space for microforms included the existence of electrical floor ducts in one end of the room. Those were installed as part of the building's original construction (occupancy was in 1967), and they served as an "anchor" for our microforms location decision. Adjacent space contained our microfilm laboratory where filming and developing services were provided.

By accepting this L-shaped space, we were somewhat in the position of "cutting the suit to fit the cloth," but the amount of available space was determined to be satisfactory for our 1971 needs and would also allow for substantial growth of collections and services. Modularity and flexibility, essential to the eventual reallocation of space and to the employment of future technologies, characterized the area and further supported our decision to use this location for microforms.

Interested readers are advised to consult Francis Spreitzer's article "Library Microform Facilities" in the July, 1976 issue of *Library Technology Reports*. Figure 4 on page 421 of the Spreitzer article is the floor plan of the microforms room at the Golda Meir Library.

Our evaluation of this space, conducted despite the fact that we were "locked into" our environment, was positive. It held a central location in the library building, one flight down from the main entrance and the Reference Department. The access is easy and convenient, and an elevator is available for handicapped patrons. There is no harmful, direct light from exterior windows because the room is windowless. However, a few steps places one near a window with an outside view, and the glass front wall of the microforms room prevents a closed-in or dungeon-like atmosphere. Lighting fixtures were satisfactory with fluorescent tubes and controls that permit staff to dim light levels or to turn off lights in sections of the room. The room is carpeted, which offsets the cold, clangorous, and metallic atmosphere that is seemingly unavoidable in the typical microforms environment with its metal shelves, metal cabinets, and metal and plastic readers and reader-printers.

An atmosphere that is warm and inviting is enhanced by the room's use of natural wood millwork and the earth tones of brick walls and brick columns. In short, the location and the esthetics were advantageous. Air conditioning and the potential for microforms display and exhibit space were additional pluses.

There were two disadvantages. The construction of a new stairwell, required by fire code, deducted several hundred square feet of floor space and imposed unanticipated space-assignment problems. A satisfactory solution was later found in the ingenious placement of shelving around the

Figure 3. Entrance to Microforms Facility of the Golda Meir Library at the University of Wisconsin-Milwaukee.

enclosed stairwell. That shelving is used for the housing of boxed collections of microprint. The location of a staff lounge adjacent to the microfilm room posed a more difficult problem, and one that could not be solved architecturally. The offending space has been retained as a staff lounge, and the anticipated problems that might result from microforms having a potentially boisterous neighbor have never proven severe thanks to library staff sensitivity and cooperation. It is hoped that the staff lounge can be relocated as part of construction of the building's third stage, and the space now assigned to the lounge can then become available for expansion of the microforms facility. At present, the microforms room houses UWM's entire microforms collection (more than 841,000 items) less the ERIC files. It is expected that we can house upwards of 1.25 million microforms in this area before we are required to expand into additional floor space.

I am not a microforms specialist, and I do not intend to masquerade in those purple robes. My approach to the design of a microforms facility and the selection of furnishings and equipment was that of a library administrator. My overriding considerations were, therefore, costs, user services, and staff efficiencies. One question that was repeatedly addressed in our planning was the effect of our suggestions upon the microforms user.

Cost dictated minimal room remodeling. Carpeting, light fixtures, walls, and columns would not be changed. No new walls, save for the entranceway, would be constructed. The entrance would be glass with the warmth of quarter-sliced, stained oak framing and doors. Microforms are frequently seen by the uninitiated library patron as austere, formidable, confusing, intimidating, frustrating, and frightening, and, understandably, many students, and more faculty than we care to admit, avoid using them.

I felt that a glass-walled entrance, inviting the user's gaze and, hopefully, his presence in the microforms room would help to overcome user apprehensions regarding microformats. A "clean" set of identifying graphics is represented by a lighted MICROFORMS sign over the door identifying the room. An engraved statement of service hours is permanently affixed to the door; handlettered signs are not used.

An arrangement of microfilm carrels to the left and right of the entrance draws the user to the centrally situated service desk, which is staffed during all hours of service and which is clearly marked MICROFORMS INFORMATION. The service desk is placed in front of the open access microforms storage area. To the left of the desk is shelving for indexes, guides, and reference materials. This placement brings the inquiring patron and the on-duty staff member together in proximity to the collection and to any reference tools or location guides that they might need. A central corridor, of adequate width to preclude a feeling of being overcrowded, allows for traffic flow and for the placement of several large, round reading tables, which are reserved for use by microforms users. The north end of the room (at the top of Spreitzer's floor plan) is the area that has floor electrical conduits, and we have placed all reader-printers and all microfiche, microcard, and microprint readers on open, library reading tables in this space.

We decided against the provision of individual carrels or cubicles in this area in order to retain openness, to maintain a feeling of spaciousness, and to hold down remodeling costs. The reactions from users and from staff have been favorable, and that is, in part, because of our ability to control lighting levels in order to facilitate improved images on viewer screens.

I am not going to attempt to rewrite or paraphrase the excellent material on the selection of micrographics equipment that has been prepared by microform specialists. This is readily available to the interested reader. However, I will share several of the major criteria for the selection of equipment at the Golda Meir Library. In 1971, our microforms collection was predominantly microfilm on reels, and we first sought to increase the number of microfilm readers. (The budget permitted the eventual purchase of eighteen microfilm readers.) We wanted a reader that would provide a good viewing image, ease of operation, trouble-free and reliable performance, and an operating mechanism that would not scratch or damage our film in transporting it past the lens. Affordability and compatibility with the room's esthetics were additional features that we sought. The reader finally selected met to some degree all of these features and numerous other characteristics included on our specifications list, which was prepared by consulting several of the standard guides and catalogs. The microfilm readers purchased were manufactured in quarter-sliced white oak and were finished to match the room's woodwork.

New microfiche, microcard, and microprint readers were not purchased in 1971 because of the lack of machines on the market that exhibited any marked improvements over those that we owned. Budget limitations reinforced that decision, but, in the intervening years, we have replaced a number of our readers and reader-printers, and the configuration and inventory of microforms equipment held at UWM has been greatly improved since design of this facility was undertaken.

After hearing and/or reading all of the standard arguments regarding microforms in cabinets versus microforms in boxes on shelves, we chose shelving for boxed sets of microcard and microprint. Cabinets were chosen for other microcards and for all microfilm and microfiche. The cabinets are double-tiered, providing considerable additional storage space. (Our physical structure permits the stacking of microfilm cabinets. Structural considerations may require a floor load check by an architect or engineering consulting firm in some buildings, and this factor should be addressed by all microforms librarians considering that option for storage of microforms.)

All microforms at UWM are cataloged; the cards are filed in the main card catalog. Indexes to major collections are available both in the microforms room and in the general reference collection near the card catalog. Patrons needing microforms assistance may obtain that from either the Reference Department's staff or from personnel on duty in the microforms facility. The microforms facility is open and staffed from 8:00 A.M. to midnight, Monday through Thursday, 8:00 A.M. to 6:00 P.M., Friday and Saturday, and noon to midnight on Sunday, for a generous total of ninety-six hours of access each week. This complements the 7:00 A.M. to midnight weekday and 8:00 A.M. to midnight weekend service hours for the rest of the Golda Meir Library.

The availability of coin-operated microfilm copiers, which allow the microforms user self-service copying, has been an important advantage. It frees staff time, allows the user to copy precisely as he wishes, and enlists the user's sympathy, through hands-on experience, for the technical problems of copying from film and the ofttimes unsatisfactory results.

Microforms displays have been an additional bonus. They enlist readers' interest and can draw in the undergraduate student. Our various exhibits have dealt with themes (e.g., women's studies from microtext) and with microforms as a format (e.g., various kinds of microforms displayed and explained; a map of the United States with distances shown in relation to microforms: "Did you know that the Library has x miles of microfilm that would reach from Milwaukee to Omaha?")

In looking back over seven years of use of our microforms facility, I am pleased that we have experienced relatively few problems directly attributable to our design of the facility, to floor plan arrangements, to service procedures, or to equipment selection. With an open access microforms collection, file integrity will always be a concern, and staff and users must necessarily be instructed to be careful. (It should be noted that we do not encourage unrestricted patron access to the microforms files, and all refiling is performed by library staff.) Reader-printer maintenance will always be problematic for we are in large measure at the mercy of local service contracts with work performed by off-campus personnel. (I cannot be anything but pessimistic on that subject.) The indexing of microforms has always been less than it might be, and librarians and microforms user complaints are heard on that score. That, too, is beyond our control.

Several years ago, in a move motivated by, I am told, ecological and energy concerns, UWM Physical Plant personnel installed hot-air hand dryers in all restrooms in the library. This eliminated the need for paper towels. It also used up much of the building's remaining electrical power reserves and, I am now told, it will be extremely expensive for us to expand our electrical sources to support additional technology (e.g., computer terminals, micrographics equipment, etc.). It should be known that the hand dryers were installed without consultation with the librarian.

Our planning for the future of microforms collections and services at UWM must address several concerns. My colleagues and I see an increasingly important potential emerging from computer access to bibliographic databases and local availability of important, related collections in miniaturized format (e.g., subject searches, via the computer, of ERIC with the ERIC fiche available in-house; the similar services of CIS and ASI). The continuation and expansion of such computer access/microformat marriages is, at this juncture, a fiscal matter, and it must be addressed in our construction of forthcoming library budgets.

The continuing format shift of microtext that we are buying (from microfilm on reels to microfiche) will dictate a reconfiguration of micrographics equipment and storage arrangements. That, too, becomes a budgetary concern.

The preservation of microforms is a haunting question that lurks in the shadows, phantom-like, to spring out at any moment. In recognizing that only silver halide film has known archival qualities and other kinds of film possess undetermined characteristics of longevity or of deterioration, then we are, in my opinion, obliged to admit that we may be spending vast sums during the twentieth century, purchasing huge collections of microforms that will become restoration nightmares for our twenty-first-century successors. Our microforms facility at UWM provides air conditioning and humidity control levels designed at best for creature comfort. No provision has been made for a highly sophisticated storage environment. Can that, too, be contributing to the next century's problems because of too much heat, too many seasonal swings in temperature and humidity, excessive dryness during the winter heating season, and an inability to "scrub" acids and chemicals out of the circulating air?

At the 1978 meetings of the International Federation of Library Associations and Institutions in Czechoslovakia, I heard a most interesting presentation on the proper storage environment for microforms. Suggestions that were presented included the storage of all film in metal or polyester containers that do not decompose or release corrosive or oxydizing substances, the purchase of only silver halide film, absolute care in the fixing and rinsing of film, storage in strictly controlled atmospheric conditions of low temperature and humidity, and complete protection against air pollution and damage from light. These are all laudable goals, of course, but probably no academic library in the world meets these standards to any significant degree. Optimum temperature ranges recommended by the IFLA speaker were 4°C for nitrate films, 6° to 12°C for triacetate films, and below 0°C for color films. It was recognized that only security copies of great value could receive such care and that the need for recopying must inevitably be faced.

Perhaps, in the decades ahead, our successors will view today's attempts to provide microforms rooms that are convenient, inviting, efficient, and esthetically pleasing as superficial solutions that failed to address the ultimate problem, the preservation of the collections.

REFERENCES

Alsmeyer, Henry L., Jr., and West, Tawana P. "Microforms at Texas A & M University." *Microform Review* 3 (October 1974):260–262.

Armstrong, Chris. "Shipboard Libraries: A Drop in the Ocean?" *Assistant Librarian* 69 (July/August 1976):126–130.

Bansa, H. Report presented at the 44th Council Meeting of the International Federation of Library Associations and Institutions, Štrbské Pleso, Czechoslovakia, August, 1978.

Beattie, James L. "Princeton Microfilm Project." *Microform Review* 6 (March 1977):73–75.

Bechanan, H. Gordon. "The Organization of Microforms in the Library." *Library Trends* 8 (January 1960):391–406.

Beck, William L. "A Realistic Approach to Microform Management." *Microform Review* 2 (July 1973):172–176.

Butcher, Roger. "National Data on Microfiche: Bibliographic and MARC Based Use of COM." *Reprographics Quarterly* 9 (Summer 1976):104–107.

Carroll, C. Edward. "Some Problems of Microform Utilization in Large University Libraries." *Microform Review* 1 (January 1972):19–24.

Coffman, R. J. "Microform Serials Collections: A Systems Analysis." *Serials Librarian* 1 (Fall 1976):45–50.

Conference on Microfilm Utilization: The Academic Library Environment, Denver, 1970. *Microfilm Utilization: The Academic Library Environment; Report.* Denver: University of Denver, 1971.

Daghita, Joan M. "A Core Collection of Journals on Microfilm in a Community Teaching Hospital Library." *Bulletin of the Medical Library Association* 64 (April 1976):240–241.

Darling, Pamela W. "Microforms in Libraries: Preservation and Storage." *Microform Review* 5 (April 1976):93–100.

DeVilliers, Ann M., and Schloman, Barbara Frick. "Experiences with Scientific Journals on Microfilm in an Academic Reading Room." *Special Libraries* 64 (December 1973):555–560.

Diaz, Albert James, ed. *Microforms in Libraries: A Reader.* Weston, Conn.: Microform Review, 1975.

Doebler, Paul. "New Media Publishing: Coping with Microforms in Libraries." *Publishers Weekly* 208 (10 November 1975):30.

Dranov, Paula. *Microfilm: The Librarians' View, 1976–77.* White Plains, N.Y.: Knowledge Industry Publications, 1976.

Duncan, E. E. "Microfiche Collections for the New York Times/Information Bank." *Microform Review* 2 (October 1973):269–271.

Ellsworth, Ralph E. *Planning Manual for Academic Library Buildings.* Metuchen, N.J.: Scarecrow Press, 1973.

———. *Planning the College and University Library Building.* 2 ed. Boulder, Colorado: Pruett Press, 1968.

Fair, Judy, "The Microtext Reading Room: A Practical Approach." *Microform Review* 1 (July 1972):199–202.

———. "The Microtext Reading Room: Part II." *Microform Review* 1 (October 1972):269–273.

———. "The Microtext Reading Room: Part III." *Microform Review* 2 (January 1973):9–13.

———. "The Microform Reading Room: Part IV." *Microform Review* 2 (July 1973):168–171.

———. "The Microform Reading Room: Part V." *Microform Review* 3 (January 1974):11–14.

Farber, Evan Ira. "Limiting College Library Growth: Bane or Boon?" *Journal of Academic Librarianship* 1 (November 1975):12–15.

Frankenberger, Rudolf. "Mikrofichekataloge an der Universatät Augsburg." *Bibliotheksforum Bayern* 4 (1976):126–140.

Gaddy, Dale. *A Microform Handbook.* Silver Spring, Md.: National Microfilm Association, 1974.

Gardiner, E. F. "The Mitchell Library Joins B.L.C.M.P." *SLA News* 136 (November–December 1976):154–158.

"Grant to Princeton University Library." *College & Research Libraries News* 11 (December 1976):307–308.

Gray, Edward. "Microfiche for a Simultaneous Subscription: Two Experiments." *Information Revolution: Proceedings of the 38th ASIS Annual Meeting* 12 (October 26–30, 1975):95–96.

Hawken, William R. *Evaluating Microfiche Readers: A Handbook for Librarians.* Washington, D.C.: Council on Library Resources, 1975.

Heim, Kathleen M. "The Role of Microforms in the Small College Library." *Microform Review* 3 (October 1974):254–259.

Hernon, Peter. "Use of Microforms in Academic Reference Collections and Services." *Microform Review* 6 (January 1977):15–18.

Holmes, Donald C. *Determination of the Environmental Conditions Required for the Effective Utilization of Microforms.* Washington, D.C.: Association of Research Libraries, 1970.

Jebb, Marcia. "Bibliographic Control of Microforms." *Drexel Library Quarterly* 11 (October 1975):32–41.

Josephs, Melvin J. "Information Dissemination with Microforms." *IEEE Transactions on Professional Communication* PC-18 (September 1975):164–167.

LaHood, Charles G., Jr. "Selecting and Evaluating Microform Reading Equipment for Libraries." *Microform Review* 6 (March 1977):79.

Logie, Audrey. "Access to Readex Microprint U.S. Government Depository Collection." *Government Publications Review* 2 (Spring 1975):103–110.

Lyon, Cathryn C. "Some Current Uses of Microform for Scientific and Technical Research Information." *NMA Journal* 2 (Summer 1969):129–131.

Malinconico, S. Michael. "The Display Medium and the Price of the Message." *Library Journal* 101 (15 October, 1976):2144–2149.

Martin, John H. "Après le Déluge: Resuscitating a Water-logged Library." *Wilson Library Bulletin* 50 (November 1975):233–241.

McConaghey, W. C. "Basic Microfilm for the Librarian." *Illinois Libraries* 58 (March 1976):191–194.

Meadow, Charles T. "Microfilm and the Library: A Prospective." *Drexel Library Quarterly* 11 (October 1975):83–88.

Metcalf, Keyes D. *Planning Academic and Research Library Buildings.* New York: McGraw-Hill, 1965.

"A Microform Policy Statement." *APLA Bulletin* 40 (Summer 1976):29–32.

Morgan, Candace. "The User's Point of View." *Illinois Libraries* 58 (March 1976):216–219.

National Microfilm Association. *Guide to Micrographic Equipment.* Edited by Hubbard Ballou, 6th ed. Silver Spring, Md.: National Microfilm Association, 1975.

Nitsos, James L. "You're Buying a Micro-what?" *Audiovisual Instruction* 21 (October 1976):20–21.

Nutter, Susan K. "Microforms and the User: Key Variables of User Acceptance in a Library Environment." *Drexel Library Quarterly* 11 (October 1975):17–31.

Powell, D. J. "The Availability of Publications in Microform." *Reprographics Quarterly* 9 (Autumn 1976):144–147.

Powers, William J., Jr. "Purposes, Policies, Problems in Microform Usage." *Illinois Libraries* 58 (March 1976):188–191.

"Princeton University Library Receives CLR Grant." *Microform Review* 6 (January 1977):8–9.

Reed, Jutta R. "Cost Comparisons of Periodicals in Hard Copy and on Microform." *Microform Review* 5 (July 1976):185–192.

"Revised Microform Procurement Standards." *Illinois Libraries* 58 (March 1976):224–227.

Rich, Margaret. "Indexing of Serial Publications in the Readex Microprint Collection of U.S. Government Documents." *Government Publications Review* 3 (Summer 1976):109–111.

Running Out of Space—What are the Alternatives? Proceedings of the preconference, June, 1975, San Francisco, sponsored by the Buildings for College and University Libraries Committee, Buildings and Equipment Section of the American Library Administration Division, American Library Association. Gloria Novak, ed. Chicago: American Library Association, 1978.

Saffady, William. *Computer-Output Microfilm: Its Library Applications.* Chicago: American Library Association, 1978.

————. "Microfilm Equipment and Retrieval Systems for Library Picture Collections." *Special Libraries* 65 (October/November 1974):440–444.

————. *Micrographics*. Littleton, Colorado: Libraries Unlimited, 1978.

Salmon, Stephen R. "User Resistance to Microforms in the Research Library." *Microform Review* 3 (July 1974):194–199.

Schell, Hal B., ed. *Reader on the Library Building*. Reader series in Library and Information Science. Englewood, Colorado: Microcard Editions Books, 1975.

Spaulding, Carl. "The Fifty Dollar Reading Machine and Other Micromarvels." *Library Journal* 101 (15 October, 1976):2133–2138.

————. "Teaching the Use of Microfilm Readers." *Microform Review* 6 (March 1977):80–81.

Spigai, Frances G. *The Invisible Medium: The State of the Art of Microform and a Guide to the Literature*. Stanford, Calif.: ERIC Clearinghouse on Media and Technology; Washington, D.C., ERIC Clearinghouse on Library and Information Science, American Society for Information Science, 1973.

Spreitzer, Francis F. "Library Microform Facilities." *Library Technology Reports* 12 (July 1976):407–435.

Staite, Keith D. "Microforms in a College Library." *MICRODOC* 15 (1976):119–128.

Stevens, Rolland E. "Resources in Microform for the Research Library." *Microform Review* 1 (January 1972):9–18.

Styles, B. R., and Overton, C. D. "The Designer as a Problem." *Aslib Proceedings* 29 (January 1977):17–23.

Surrency, Erwin C. "Micrographic Librarianship: An Outline." *International Journal of Law Libraries* 4 (November 1976):206–215.

————. "Part IV—Library Administration of Historical Materials: Microforms." *Law Library Journal* 69 (August 1976):326–328.

Tannenbaum, Arthur C. "Human Engineering Factors Help Determine Microform Use in the Research Library." *Information Revolution: Proceedings of the 38th ASIS Annual Meeting* 12 (October 26–30, 1975):97–98.

Tannenbaum, Arthur, and Sidhom, Eva. "User Environment and Attitudes in an Academic Microform Center." *Library Journal* 101 (15 October, 1976):2139–2143.

Taylor, Desmond. "The NAPCU Microforms Center: Proposal for a Northwest Regional Microforms and Storage Center." *PNLA Quarterly* 41 (Winter 1977):4–12.

Teague, Sydney John. *Microform Librarianship*. London: Butterworths, 1977.

Thompson, Godfrey. *Planning and Design of Library Buildings*. 2nd. ed. New York: Nichols Publishing Company. 1977.

Veaner, Allen B. *The Evaluation of Micropublications: A Handbook for Librarians*. LTP Publication No. 17. Chicago: Library Technology Program, American Library Association, 1971.

————. "Microfilm and the Library: A Retrospective." *Drexel Library Quarterly* 11 (October 1975):3–16.

————. "Micropublication." In *Advances in Librarianship*, v. 2, edited by Melvin J. Voigt. New York and London: Seminar Press, 1971.

Weber, David C. "Design for a Microtext Reading-room." *UNESCO Bulletin for Libraries* 20 (November–December 1966):303–308.

Weber, Hans H. "The Librarian's View of Microforms." *IEEE Transactions on Professional Communication* PC-18 (September 1975):168–173.

Woodward, A., and Jardine, D. "Librarians' Reactions to Non-conventional Publishing Methods." In *Trends in Scholarly Publishing*. West Yorkshire: British Library, 1976.

RLIN AND OCLC—SIDE BY SIDE:
TWO COMPARISONS STUDIES

Kazuko M. Dailey, Grazia Jaroff and Diana Gray

GENERAL INTRODUCTION

Kazuko M. Dailey

The two reports which follow, "RLIN/OCLC, A Cataloging Cost Study in the Health Sciences Library," and "A Comparison of RLIN and OCLC: Hit Rate, Quality of Member Copy, and Coding," were produced solely for internal library use, and were not designed as formal scientific investigation. Their primary purpose was twofold: first, to understand clearly the difference between the two technical processing systems as applied to Davis, and secondly, to produce data that would permit future decisions regarding these systems to be based more on fact and less on assumption, however educated and widely accepted such assumptions might be. The data produced in these studies contain no major eye-openers, but surprisingly, much of the information has never appeared in the professional journals. Although the library administration of Davis is

Advances in Library Administration and Organization, volume 1, pages 69–125
ISBN: 0-89232-213-6

satisfied with the validity of the data for our situation, we wish to caution that their applicability to libraries of different sizes, varying philosophies, or alternate practices cannot be taken for granted.

The General Library of the University of California at Davis is a medium-sized research library with a total collection of 1,343,000 volumes. The library has two major branches: the Physical Sciences Library and the Health Sciences Library, which houses collections for human and animal medicine. The Health Sciences Library has its own technical processing unit, separate from the Main Library's. The Main Library, which includes the Physical Sciences Library, holds approximately 1,272,000 volumes with an annual addition of 77,000 volumes, while the Health Sciences Library has 165,000 volumes with an annual acquisition rate of 9,300 volumes. Approximately 35,000 new monographic titles are added to the Main Library, and 3,400 monographic titles are added to the Health Sciences Collections in a given year.

The history of the on-line cataloging at Davis dates back to 1977. For a variety of reasons, including a policy decision to increase monographic acquisitions in lieu of backfiles and sets, and with no increase in technical processing personnel, the library administration elected to adopt an on-line processing system to take advantage of the shared cataloging on the Research Library Information Network (RLIN), formerly BALLOTS, with two terminals located in the Main Library's Catalog Department. The Health Sciences Library was brought into RLIN in the spring of 1977, sharing the use of the two terminals in the Catalog Department of the Main Library.

After two years of cataloging on RLIN, the Health Sciences Library requested a change to OCLC, on the basis that the cataloging data of the National Library of Medicine was available on OCLC, as well as contributed catalog records from other medical libraries. At that time, the medical library of Stanford University was the only other medical research library using RLIN. The advantage of using OCLC for our Health Sciences Library seemed reasonably clear, and, accordingly, the library administration acceded to the request, with an express proviso that the OCLC cataloging operation should not incur higher costs, unless commensurate increases in service accompanied the raise in charges, and that the OCLC system be as cost-effective as the operation under RLIN. As a result of these two specific requirements, the head of the Health Sciences Library requested a comparative study of RLIN and OCLC in the summer of 1979. Grazia Jaroff, an administrative analyst, designed the study and collected data for the RLIN operation before the advent of OCLC. The data for the OCLC portion was collected six months after that system was installed. Her work resulted in the study, "RLIN/OCLC, A Cataloging Cost Study."

The second study, "Comparison of RLIN and OCLC: Hit Rate, Quality of Member Copy and Coding," was an outcome of quite another set of circumstances. As indicated earlier, Davis's use of RLIN goes back more than four years. From the very begining of the operation, the system received very high marks from the staffs of the Acquisitions and Catalog Departments. The effectiveness of RLIN for bibliographic verification was demonstrated by the Acquisitions Department in a marked increase in productivity of the bibliographic checkers shortly after the introduction of RLIN. In the Catalog Department, however, a rise in productivity was not visible in the first year, but from the second year on cataloging productivity accelerated at the rate of approximately 10% a year, until the advent of AACR2 in 1981. We know that the additional cataloging procedures attendant upon the adoption of AACR2 will impact on our cataloging productivity but how effectively OCLC and RLIN will respond to the requirements of AACR2 in a comparative sense is an area of study yet to be done.

When RLIN had gained staff approval and increased productivity, the library administration was content to let sleeping dogs lie, but on several occasions we were called on to provide reasons for our choice of a database. Thus, with the appearance of OCLC terminals in the library for a major retrospective conversion project in the fall of 1980, the opportunity arose to operate the two systems side by side, to make comparisons, and to determine whether our observations and assumptions about the comparative advantages of RLIN were in fact correct. Diana Gray, coordinator for RLIN operations in the Main Library, and supervisor of the retrospective conversion unit, was asked to undertake the comparative study. The original plan included three major parts, comparative assessment of (1) pre-order searching and search for copy with book in hand, (2) the quality of member-contributed copy, and (3) catalog maintenance activities. As of this writing, the final section on catalog maintenance activities, though of major importance, has not been completed. That study will be carried out over the next few months.

There is no ideal time to do a comparative study of OCLC and RLIN, for the two systems are constantly evolving. For instance, the two studies are at variance in regard to the time required to search in OCLC. In one case, OCLC took longer than RLIN, while in the other test, there was little difference between the two. That discrepancy is probably the result of the search enhancement that OCLC introduced in the fall of 1980, the period between the two surveys, but we cannot document that situation. Similarly, the test on the quality of member copy was completed before OCLC implemented the global change of headings from AACR1 to AACR2 state in December 1980. If the test had been conducted after the changeover, the data would have contained another dimension to be analyzed, and the job of comparing the records of the two utilities would have been made more complicated.

At the time the data were collected for the Gray study, only about half of the Research Library Group (RLG) members were actually cataloging in RLIN. Therefore, when all current members are fully on-line, and their archives files are loaded into RLIN, it is not unreasonable to suppose that the database will be significantly richer than it is today. Furthermore, RLIN's near term development includes the installation of an authority control system and a reconfigured database, which will permit menu mode of display and would, presumably, make searching far more efficient. How these system modifications will affect the user's mode of operation is, of course, impossible to predict.

In the same vein, the on-line availability of LC-name-authority data to OCLC users may already have brought about some improvement in the use of authorized names in member-contributed records. On the other hand, the mismatch between card catalog information which is in pre-AACR2 state and the database information which is in AACR2 may present problems which will require modifications to the cataloging and searching procedures. For the select few libraries which have abandoned the card catalog as the primary access to the library collection, the changeover probably does not present a problem.

Thus, if our tests were to be duplicated today, there would be, inevitably, some data that would contradict our report. On the other hand, there are other data that are not subject to the kinds of changes discussed above. By and large, intellectual activities, such as detailed subject analysis and assignment of specific subject headings, the level of encoding, and the accurate use of MARC format, are hardly affected by these changes. Therefore, the results of our study in these aspects may continue to have validity for some time.

As is to be expected, the two comparative studies performed at Davis were tailored for our situations—our requirements were made the criteria against which the system's performance, capabilities, and qualities were judged. Even between the Health Sciences Library and the Main Library, requirements are sufficiently different as to allow for the possibility that one system may be suitable for Main but not for H.S.L. The Jaroff study was done in a small medical library technical processing environment in which there was relatively little flexibility and even less task specialization. If the Jaroff test had been applied to the Main Library in which staff cataloging is divided into levels of difficulty and each level pegged at an appropriate staff classification, it would have yielded a set of data quite unlike those contained in the Jaroff paper. In interpreting the data gathered, readers should be guided by the priorities and needs of their particular library.

As a reading of the Gray paper will make clear, a research library orientation figured prominently in the point of view of the study. Our insistence that coding be complete and accurate, for instance, may appear needlessly fussy to nonresearch institutions. Since, however, we anticipate shortly an on-line catalog in which coded information will be used in searching, we regard coding, as do most other research libraries, as an important element of the machine record. Other such specific concerns could be cited and again readers are cautioned to be wary of direct application of our finding to their own environments.

Despite these caveats and the need to exercise care in using the data we have developed, we believe that our studies lead to explicit statements about the strengths and shortcomings of the systems. Our conclusions are not original; rather, they are restatements, as it were, of assumptions which have often been advanced but without documentary support. By making our internal documents available to the profession, we hope to encourage other libraries to come forth with their analyses of the bibliographic utilities and to perform analyses, where before we have had only assertions or assumptions. The ultimate purpose of "going public" is not to criticize, but to comprehend the bibliographic databases, OCLC or RLIN. We believe it is essential that we have clear understanding of the differences between the utilities and how those differences affect our current operations and the shape of our future catalogs. With libraries, it is axiomatic that what we do today will influence future scholars in their use of library resources.

In order to aid the reader, we provide the following list of Davis abbreviations and acronyms which are used throughout the text of the two papers.

TERMS USED

AACR2	Anglo American Cataloging Rules—2nd Edition
CATLINE	CATalog-on-LINE, a National Library of Medicine database
CDF	Catalog Data File
CIP	Cataloging in Publication
CLSI	CL Systems, Inc., a library circulation system
Firm Order	An order placed for a specific item. The term is used to distinguish regular orders from approval plan receipts.
FMRC	Full MARC record
HSL	Health Science Library, University of California, Davis
HSTS	Health Sciences Technical Services, HSL, UCD
IPF	In-Process File
LA	Library Assistant

LCCN   Library of Congress Classification Number
LCSH   Library of Congress Subject Headings
MOF   Multiple Order Form
NAF   Name Authority File
NAL   National Agricultural Library
NLM   National Library of Medicine
NUC   National Union Catalog
OCLC   Online Computer Library Center, formerly OCLC, Inc.,
          formerly Ohio College Library Center
ORC   Order Request Card
RLG   Research Libraries Group
RLIN   Research Libraries Information Network

RLIN/OCLC CATALOGING COST STUDY IN THE HEALTH SCIENCES LIBRARY

Grazia Jaroff

I. INTRODUCTION

This study will compare cataloging costs incurred by the Health Sciences Library (HSL), University of California, Davis, under two technical processing systems: RLIN and OCLC. Until January 1980, the Health Sciences Technical Services units used the RLIN data base, which was accessed through terminals installed at the Peter J. Shields Library located about a mile away, for cataloging and card production. Pre-order searches, with printing of catalog copy, were completed on all non-serial titles. After receipt of the material, pre-cataloging searches were repeated, at intervals of up to six months, in an attempt to obtain both MARC and NLM catalog copy. HSL needs National Library of Medicine (NLM) subject headings and call numbers in order to provide its patrons with a unified approach to biomedical information sources. At the completion of the cataloging process, a copy was input into the database and cards ordered. Maintenance activities were performed as needed.

In May of 1979, anticipating the advent of OCLC in HSL, originally scheduled for the end of October 1979, the Library Administration resolved that, (1) the cost of cataloging should not increase unless services were enhanced or added, and (2) the OCLC operation should be as cost-effective as possible. A cost study was authorized with these specific charges:

Identify the cataloging costs with use of RLIN
Identify the same costs with the use of OCLC, when installed
Compare the operations and services rendered

The library already collects an impressive array of workload statistics, as well as detailed cost figures in its budgets, but comparisons between alternate processes cannot be readily made since task-level cost information is not maintained.

Given the high expense and time-consuming nature of data collection and analysis, the axiom was adopted that "[data collection and analysis] should be limited to those activities which are change candidates."[1] After an examination of the existing literature on other libraries' experiences and evaluations of RLIN and OCLC products and services, possible impact points were identified and those operations which were subject to potential change were isolated accordingly. The following elements were selected for scrutiny:

Cataloging process:
Processing time per unit of work—single and in the aggregate
Cost per unit processed—single and in the aggregate
Processing time elapsed in working days
Staff utilization

Cataloging Services:
Comparable direct costs
Hit rates

Those measurable variables which impinge upon direct cost, labor costs in particular, were the major concern. Turnaround (or processing) time was included because it is equally important in the HSL context. RLIN procedures were described and timed between July 1979 and January 1980. OCLC operations were timed between May and July in order to allow for six months of staff training time after the terminals were installed in early 1980.

The data gathered from RLIN and OCLC are summarized in Section II, Cataloging Process below. The analysis of the data are presented in Section III. Although only the RLIN portion of the study was performed, since it is a critical element of the HSL operation, the result of the processing Time Lag investigation is included in this paper as Section IV. Some final conclusions drawn from the study are presented in Section V.

A. Techniques used

The RLIN searching/cataloging/post-cataloging process, began with the identification of functions, tasks and activities which appeared to be change candidates, essentially following the methodology and general guidelines set by Jaffe, Mitchell and Tanis in their *Cost Analysis of Library Functions.*[2] As they suggested, activities too small to be timed were combined, when logical and possible. Not included in the study were items such as the filing of cards into the shelf list and main card catalog, because no major changes were anticipated. The cataloging of serials was also excluded since serials were not being processed by RLIN during the study.

The entire workload for each activity was sampled at each work station, by timing the batches of material going through the steps. Data collection periods varied from a few weeks, for continuous tasks, to several months, for tasks of cyclical nature or those which occurred less frequently. We timed a minimum of three samples batches for each activity with a few exceptions. The work unit was defined as a title.

The main data collection technique used was the "diary method" which yields information on unit times and staff costs: each staff member noted the beginning and ending time of a unique activity in relation to volumes processed.[3] The major pitfall of the standard diary method, inflated data span, was minimized by limiting the self-timing to specific activities. The value of the "informal recall" approach was included by allowing staff members to indicate a modification to average unit times, to compensate for unusual circumstances.[4] Logs were used in several instances to measure processing times in working days. The same format and data collection methods were followed in describing the process under OCLC.

By computing the average unit time and average personnel cost of each task performed under both cataloging systems, comparable sample figures were obtained which point to those processing steps where appreciable differences reside. The risk of this approach, namely that of overlooking a task which may be significant on a different system was recognized, but a complete cataloging study was impractical in terms of time, cost, effort and disruption. Reliability checks were made on the data collected by comparing figures to other departmental or standard statistics and, occasionally, by retiming batches of tasks which had returned seemingly exceptional results. In such cases, explanatory notes have been added to the tables.

B. Costs

Only direct costs were considered, such as personnel, machine time and services, and special supplies. The use of administrative and facilities overhead in comparing costs is discounted in similar library studies as being purely academic.[5] Therefore, support services such as accounting, personnel, library administration, and building costs such as maintenance, electricity and space, were disregarded.

C. *Personnel*

A simple comparison of unit time per task would ignore the shifting of activities among differing personnel levels, which may turn out to be significant on a different system. The shifting to higher-, or lower-paid personnel is reflected by the calculation of personnel costs per unit.

Personnel costs are expressed in standard unit costs, whch include a 30% increment for fringe benefits and nonproductive time: sick leave, vacation, breaks, personal time, delays and fatigue factors.[6] Calculations are based on January 1980 average hourly rate for the position at the step 3 figure, rather than on the actual salary of each individual, and are therefore not to be taken as absolute costs, but only as units of comparison.

II. CATALOGING PROCESS

A. *Cataloging with RLIN and OCLC.*

Tables 1 through 5, itemize tasks and activities of five major processing functions as defined and timed by the people responsible for their completion, and give average unit times and personnel costs per unit of work on both systems. Measures of time are given in seconds (e.g. 26" means 26 seconds) and, occasionally in minutes and seconds (e.g. 6'38" means 6 minutes and 38 seconds). Travel time to gain access to RLIN terminals, was ignored. Personnel costs include all time spent by staff on processing routines, be they manual or machine processes. Machine costs will be covered in the analysis section of this study under D. Cataloging Services. Serials were excluded because they were not processed through RLIN at the time of sampling and no comparison could have been made. It is possible that a serial may have appeared during unit counting for some of the OCLC samples, but the impact of such an instance is insignificant.

In instances where tasks were performed only on a portion of the workload, times and costs have been adjusted accordingly and the tables annotated. An example in the CATLINE search on Table 2: All titles were searched in CATLINE under the RLIN system; on OCLC CATLINE is searched only when NLM copy is not available, namely on 83% of the titles searched.

Table 1. Function 1. Pre-Order Search

RLIN

Task #	Task Description	Date of Sample	# of Batches Sampled	# of work Units in Sample	Average time per unit in Seconds	# of Hits	% of Hits	Personnel Level	Personnel Cost Per Unit	Personnel Cost Per Hit	Notes
1.	ORC in hand; batched every 2-3 days Search on terminal by one or more access points: LC # Title ISBN Corporate Name Personal Name Print results	July 79	6	169	36"	98	58	LA II	$.08	$.14	
2.	Manual Handling of RLIN print-out Underline LC # Cut & divide print-out Match ORC to print-out Revise/Retype ORC Annotate/Stamp ORC	July 79	6	169	51"			LA II	.11		
3.	Revision of tasks # 1 & 2 Match to print-out/correct Check search record Revise/suggest other searches; return	July 79	3	80	26¼"			LA III	.07		
4.	Receipt of piece; match to ORC; If discrepancy look at RLIN print-out; resolve minor differences; send to problem routine	Mar/Ap 80*	11	48	51"			LA I	.09		
5.	Additional searches for "originals" (No matches, no RLIN) including BiP, BNB.	Mar/Ap 80*	11	7	193"			LA I	.35		13% of receipts

*Original samples for tasks 4 and 5, taken in July 1979, were thrown out as we discovered only "originals" had been timed. Sample retaken on RLIN in March/April 1980.

78

OCLC

Firm Orders Task #	Approval Plan Task #	Task Description	Type of order	Date of Sample	# of Batches Sampled	# of work Units in Sample	Average time per unit in Seconds	# of Hits	% of Hits	Personnel Level	Personnel Cost Per Unit	Personnel Cost Per Hit
1.	1.	ORC in hand (Batched every 2–3 days) Search on terminal by one or more access points:										
		ISBN/ISSN	Approval plan	May–June 80	7	138	104″	122	88	LA I	$.19	$.22
			Firm; GE; Cat Seps	May–June 80	11	198	112″	126	64	LA II	.24	.38
		LC card number	Firm orders only	May–June 80	2	45	87″	34	75	LA III	.22	.29
		Title										
		Corporate/Personal Name										
		Print desired copy/copies	Combined averages			381	106″	282	74		.22	.30
2.	2.	Manual Handling of Print-out Underline type of copy (040 field)	Approval plan	May–June 80	7	138	94″			LA I	.17	
			Firm; GE; Cat Seps									
		Cut and divide print-out	Firm orders only	May–June 80	11	198	42″			LA II	.09	
		Match ORC to print-out	Combined averages	May–June 80	2	45	60″			LA III	.15	
		Revise/retype ORC					63″				.13	
		Annotate/Stamp ORC										
3.		Revision of tasks 1. and 2. for outgoing firm orders Match to print-out/correct/return	Firm orders	May–June 80	5	150	37″			LA III	.09	
4.		Receipt of pieces from orders out Match to ORC; resolve minor differences	Firm orders	May–June 80	6	123	66″			LA I	.12	
5.		For all pieces from 4., if differences/problems or no print-out, Re-search on terminal; sources: BIP, BNB, etc.	Firm orders	May–June 80	6	6*	500″			LA I	.92	

*5% of receipts

79

Table 2. Function 2. Precataloging Search

RLIN

Task #	Task Description	Date of Sample	# of Batches Sampled	# of work Units in Sample	Average time per unit in Seconds	Personnel Level	Personnel Cost Per Unit	# of Hits	% of Hits	Personnel Cost Per Hit
1.	Receiving: Compare MOF to title page / Compare ORC to title / Annotate ORC with LC #, ISBN #, etc. / Attach ORC to copy	Aug. 79	4	248	49″	LA II	$.11			
2.	Count, stamp: Count categories and record statistics, Date Stamp on ORC	Aug. 79	4	248	14″	LA II	.03			
3.	Sort for searching: LC; CDF; No Copy; CIP Tasks 1–3 combined	Aug. 79	4	213	5″ / 68″	LA II	.01 / .15			
4.	Search in RLIN Batch by Batch from 1st search through "6 months held"	Aug. 79	4	135	26″	LA II	.06	32	24	$.24
5.	Cut, Sort, Stamp RLIN searches	Aug. 79	4	135	15″	LA II	.03			
6.	Search in CATLINE Batch by Batch from 1st search through "6 months held"	Aug. 79	4	225	32″	LA II	.07	121	54	.13
7.	Cut, Sort, Stamp CATLINE searches	Aug. 79	4	225	14″	LA II	.03			

OCLC

Task #	Task Description	Date of Sample	# of Batches Sampled	# of work Units in Sample	Average time per unit in Seconds	Personnel Level	Personnel Cost Per Unit	# of Hits	% of Hits	Personnel Cost Per Hit
1.	Receiving: Compare MOF to title page Compare ORC to title Annotate ORC with LC #, ISNB #, etc. Attach ORC to copy									
2.	Count and stamp: Count categories and record statistics, Date stamp ORC	July 80	5	261	113"	LA II	$.24			
3.	Sort for searching: OCLC, in all cases CATLINE, if no NLM found Manual NUC and NLM catalogs, if no LC and pre '72									
4.	Search OCLC: Daily receipts are searched daily First month holds, searched twice per month Sixth month holds, search once a month	July 80	24	403	74"	LA II	.16	131	32	$.49
5.	Count, stamp "no hits", forward to Hold Box or CATLINE search Cut copy for "hits", match and clip to ORC, count, forward to CATLINE search or to catalogers	July 80	11	427	34"	LA II	.07			
6.	Search in CATLINE, batches: one month holds, six months holds, "ready to go"	July 80	11	313	35"*	LA II	.06	101	32	.28
7.	Stamp, cut CATLINE searches and forward to catalogers	July 80	8	224	20"*	LA II	.04			

*83% of receipts

81

Table 3. Function 3. Copy-Cataloging

RLIN
All Samples Combined: 121 units

Sample #	Date of Sample	Units Completed	Average time per unit in Minutes and Seconds	Unit Times Low	Unit Times High	Personnel Level	Cost Per Unit	Unit Costs Low	Unit Costs High
1	Sept. 11–20; Oct. 23	84	9'12"	3'	24'	LA III	$1.38	$.45	$3.60
2	Dec. 13–26	21	7'28"	4'	20'	LA III	1.12	.60	3.00
3	Dec. 26–Jan. 14	16	8'41"	5'	20'	LA III	1.30	.75	3.00
All	Average for combined samples	121	8'50'	3'	24'	LA III	1.32	.45	3.60

Task Description	Task Frequency	% of task Frequency to total units
Match card copy to piece	120	99
Alter, complete CIP	52	42
Annotate slips, ORC	121	100
Verify call number	111	91
File shelf list stopper	120	99
Maintenance slip	—	—
Subjects & Call # Changes on LC	109	90
Verify names/NAF	10	8
Change of entry	5	4
Subject change a 1st edition	—	—
Retrieve book for analytics	—	—
Series/congress check	5	4
Type worksheet	3	2

OCLC

All Samples Combined: 128 units

Task Description	Task Frequency	% of task Frequency to total units	Sample #	Date of Sample	Units Completed	Average time per unit in Minutes and Seconds	Unit Times		Personnel Level	Cost Per Unit	Unit Costs	
							Low	High			Low	High
Match card copy to piece	128	100	1	Mar. 11–May 7	50	9'30"	5'	55'	LA III	$1.43	$.75	$8.25
Alter, complete CIP, code	79	61	2	May 14–June 2	42	6'58"	4'	20'	LA III	1.05	.60	3.00
Annotate slips, ORC	128	100	3	June 3–July 2	36	9' 7"	4'	20'	LA III	1.37	.60	3.00
Verify call number	125	98	All	Average for combined samples	128	8'33"	4'	55'	LA III	1.28	.60	8.25
File shelf list stopper	128	100										
Maintenance slip	—	—										
Subjects & Call # Changes on LC	125	98										
Verify names/NAF	7	5										
Change of entry	7	5										
Subject change a 1st edition	1	8										
Retrieve book for analytics	—	—										
Series/congress check	10	8										
Type worksheet	—	—										
Error report	3	2										

Table 4. Function 4. Full Cataloging

RLIN

All Samples Combined: 74 units

Task Description	Task Frequency	% of Total Units Completed	Sample #	Date of Sample	Units Completed	Average time per unit in Minutes and Seconds	Unit times Low	Unit times High	Personnel Level	Cost Per Unit	Unit Costs Low	Unit Costs High
Descriptive Cataloging	68	92	1	Oct. 79	48	13'38"	9'	23'30"	Assoc. Lib	$3.00	$1.98	$5.17
Classification Work	39	53	2	Nov. 79	17	11'53"	8'	24'	Assoc. Lib	2.61	1.76	5.28
Subject Work	42	57	3	Dec. 79	9	15'26"	10'	23'	Assoc. Lib	3.39	2.20	5.06
Name, Main, Added Entry Work	22	30	Combined	Oct.–Dec. 79	74	13'27"	8'	24'	Assoc. Lib	2.96	1.76	5.28
Change of entry	8	11										

OCLC

All Samples Combined: 133 units

Task Description	Task Frequency	% of Total Units Completed	Sample #	Date of Sample	Units Completed	Average time per unit in Minutes and Seconds	Unit times Low	Unit times High	Personnel Level	Cost Per Unit	Unit Costs Low	Unit Costs High
Descriptive Cataloging	113	85	1	Mar. 80	29	12'29"	4'	34'	Assoc. Lib	$2.75	$.88	$7.48
Classification Work	47	35	2	Apr. 1–11, 80	53	14'41"	4'	35'	Assoc. Lib	3.23	.88	7.70
Subject Work	75	56	3	Apr. 14–21, 80	51	16'33"	4'	65'	Assoc. Lib	3.64	.88	14.30
Name, Main, Added Entry Work	73	54	Combined	Mar.–Apr. 80	133	14'15"	4'	65'	Assoc. Lib	3.13	.88	14.30
Change of entry	22	17										
Coding	130	98										

Table 5. Function 5. Post-Cataloging

RLIN

Task #	Task Description	Date of Sample	# of Batches Sampled	# of Units in Sample	Average time per unit in Min & Seconds	Personnel Level	Personnel Cost Per Unit	Total Cost for "Originals"	Total cost for "In House" Type	Total Cost for "Copy"
1.	(Received Book Truck)									
	Pull covers and slips	Jan. 80	3	89	40"	LA I	$ .07			
	Type book tags	Jan. 80	3	89	1'11"	LA I	.13	$ .57	$ .57	$ .57
	Revise	Jan. 80	3	76	32"	LA I	.06			
2.	Type selin label & apply	Jan. 80	3	65	1'14"	Clerk	.12			
	Paste date due slip & tag									
	Ownership stamp									
3.	Revise: match book to work slip	Jan. 80	3	90	1'17"	LA III	.19			
	Add no. of cards needed to each set									
	Pull green slip for filing: sort slips									
4.	RLIN original input: (New to RLIN)									
	Code worksheet	1979	N.A.*	N.A.	2'30"	LA III	.38	.38		
	Input into RLIN; order cards	1979	N.A.**	N.A.	7'	LA III	1.05	1.05		
	Match & revise cards, pencil, stamp, separate by categories & disperse.	Jan. 80	3	113	2'47"	LA III	.42	.42		
5.	Original "In-house type" (Serials; Non-roman & other types not in RLIN)									
	Type card. store for duplication	Jan. 80	2	42	7' 8"	LA I	.79		.79	
	Paste on mat; file slip; receive & cut up	Jan. 80	2	40	1'	LA I	.11		.11	
	Match to workslip	Jan. 80	2	40	15"	LA I	.03		.03	
	Type card set	Jan. 80	2	42	3'	LA I	.33		.33	
	Revise, annotate, disperse	Jan. 80	3	140	28"	LA III	.07		.07	
6.	RLIN "Changes" (adding our holdings to RLIN record; minor local changes)									
	Prepare	Jan. 80	3	86	1'24"	LA I	.15			.15
	Input	Jan. 80	4	187	2'52"	LA I	.32			.32
	File	Jan. 80	3	187	9"	LA I	.02			.02
	Revise	Jan. 80	3	113	2'47"	LA III	.42			.42
	Type subjects	Jan. 80	3	185	6'***	LA I	.01			.01
								$2.42	$1.90	$1.49

*Average of trained coder timed for ACE study 1979, and person in training, Jan. 80.

**Average of sample months in 1979.

***Represents 23.5% of average time since 23.5% of sets require subject typing.

Table 5 (Continued)

OCLC

Task #	Task Description	Date of Sample	# of Batches Sampled	# of Units in Sample	Average time per unit in Min & Seconds	Personnel Level	Personnel Cost Per Unit	Total Cost for "Originals"	Total Cost for "Copy"
1.	(Received Book Truck) Pull covers Pull slips (leaving originals on truck) scan for possible questions	June 80	3	65	1'14"	LA I	$ .14	$ .14	$ .14
2.	Input in OCLC local fields from worksheet Store records in SAVE FILE	June 80	4	261	5"29"	LA I	.60		.60
2.a	Search and input originals in OCLC Store records in SAVE FILE	July 80	4	17	19'39"	LA III	2.95	2.95	
3.	Key in, on printer, call no. & M.E. to produce Book Tags, Book Labels, Call No. Labels	June 80	7	151	2' 7"	LA I	.23	.23	.23
4.	Book Processing Match book on truck to computer output, to slips Paste in: Security Tag; Book Tag; Book Label; Date Due Slip; Call No. Stamp ownership	June 80	5	208	1'14"	Clerk	.12	.12	.12
5.	Revise "changes" in SAVE FILE, within 7 days Read changes made to record; Order cards	July 80	10	228	2'	LA III	.30		.30
5.a	Search and Revise originals in SAVE FILE, within 7 days Read input, order cards	July 80	3	164	1'53"	Assoc. Lib.	.42	.42	
6.	Revise book labels and tags	July 80	5	119	1'17"	LA III	.19	.19	.19
7.	Revise cards received in weekly batches Match M.E., call no., annotate, disperse	July 80	5	225	1'53"	LA III	.28	.28	.28
								$4.33	$1.86

86

III. ANALYSIS

A. Cataloging Process

1. Pre-Order Search—Personnel Costs Summary and Comparison. By May 1980, the pre-order search workload had been divided according to type of order (Approval Plan; Firm Orders; Gifts and Exchanges; monographs in series cataloged separately), and two people were searching, instead of one, under RLIN, but tasks remained essentially the same. A straight comparison by task and totals is therefore appropriate.

Table 6. Pre-Order Search

Task #		RLIN Average		OCLC Average	
		time	cost	time	cost
1	Terminal search	36″	.08	106″	.22
2	Print-out processing	51″	.11	63″	.13
3	Revision of 1 & 2	26″	.07	37″	.09
4	Receipt of piece	51″	.09	66″	.12
	Totals for "copy"	164″	.35	272″	.56
5	Additional searches on "originals"	193″	.35 (13%)	500″	.92 (5%)
	Total for "originals"	357″	.70	772″	1.48

Several factors contribute to the difference in times and costs for Tasks 1–5:

Task #1—RLIN "automatic print" response to the search key consumed about one second and required no decision by the searcher, unless a complicated search was involved. The absence of an automatic print option in OCLC places the searcher in a decision process which requires several seconds. OCLC responds to a search with either a screen display of LC copy, in which case the searcher must request a print, or with a menu screen, in which case the searcher must choose the record(s) for display first, and then for printing.

Task #2—All duplicate records were printed and reported to OCLC during the sample time May–June 1980. This procedure was later found unnecessary and dropped, but could have inflated the sample times slightly.

Task #3—RLIN gave a printed record of the searcher's strategy, which could be evaluated by a supervisor. The OCLC system does not generate a paper record so that less revision work is required or, indeed, possible. In HSL, the revisor often does ask: "Did you search by. . . ?

or by. . . ?" or: "Why not try searching by . . . ?" There are possible implications here for training and training follow-up, employees evaluations, quality of search, number of hits, particularly for new or lower level employees.

Task #4—RLIN searches were always performed in batches. The easy in-house access to OCLC terminals encourages the searching of individual items separately, which tends to increase average time.

Task #5— The relative speed of the printer terminals used was considered as a factor affecting sample times. However, as it turned out, RLIN had the slower terminal, TI 725 at 30 cps, while OCLC printers worked at 55 cps (Diablo 820) and 120 cps, (TI Omni 800). If terminal speed had remained constant, the OCLC searching process might have taken even longer.

The task of performing additional searches on "originals" affords an interesting comparison. For each 100 titles received, 5 required extra searching on OCLC @ $.92 each = $4.60. On RLIN, for each 100 titles, 13 required additional searching, @ $.35 each = $4.55. It appears that, at least for this task, searching advantages of one system are exactly offset by those of the other.

Another point to be mentioned in connection with pre-order searching is the difference between exact and near matches. We started out timing all steps taken in each case under both systems, only to find out that the difference was too minute to count. Exact matches and copy with minor modifications needed on slips were, therefore, lumped together on both systems.

2.   Pre-cataloging Search-Personnel Costs Summary and Comparison. Tasks considered here remained stable enough to be compared below:

Table 7.   Pre-Cataloging Search

Task #		RLIN Average		OCLC Average	
		time	*cost*	*time*	*cost*
1	Receipt	49″	.11		
2	Count & Stamp	14″	.03		
3	Sort	5″	.01		
	1–3 Totals	68″	.15	113″	.24
4	Terminal search	26″	.06	74″	.16
5	Cut, sort, stamp paper output	15″	.03	34″	.07
6	Search CATLINE	32″	.07	35″	.06
7	Cut, sort, stamp CATLINE paper output	14″	.03	20″	.04
	Totals	155″	.34	276″	.57

In addition to those factors described in the analysis of Pre-order Search, higher OCLC times could be partially due to a new Pre-cataloger in training and to new methods of dealing with OCLC products still being experimented with during the sampling. Tasks 1–3, for example, could not be timed separately without substantially lengthening the process. Also, the availability of NLM copy in OCLC introduced minor changes in sorting and batching which may account for some variation. To satisfy this point, in October 1980 an additional sample of the sorting and paper handling tasks was taken, namely Tasks 3 and 5. While this sample produced lower times than the July sample, the results were still higher in OCLC than RLIN:

	New OCLC October sample	*RLIN*
Task 3 Sort for search	11½″ per unit	5″
Task 5 Cut, sort, stamp paper output	18″ per unit	15″

Since more OCLC and NLM "copy" is available at pre-order search, the items to be searched at the pre-cataloging point are fewer but more complex, compared to RLIN. This situation may be responsible for the significantly longer time required on OCLC.

3. Copy-Cataloging—Personnel Cost Summary and Comparison. Copy-cataloging tasks remained unchanged with one exception: coding

Table 8.   Copy-Cataloging Tasks

Task #	Task Description	% of Copy-Cataloging Task Frequency To Total Units	
		RLIN	*OCLC*
1	Match card copy to piece	99	100
2	Alter, complete CIP	42	—
	Alter, complete CIP, code changes	—	61
3	Annotate slips, ORC	100	100
4	Verify call number	91	98
5	File pink	99	100
6	Maintenance slip	—	—
7	Subjects & Call # Changes on LC	90	98
8	Verify names/NAF	8	5
9	Change of entry	4	5
10	Subject change a 1st edition	—	8
11	Retrieve book for analytics	—	—
12	Series/congress check	4	8
13	Type worksheet	2	—
14	Error report	—	2

for database input was added to Task 2. The term "coding" is broadly defined here to include tagging, the assignment of subfield values, as well as determining the contents of fixed and variable fields. On RLIN a staff member did all or most of the coding for input as part of the post-cataloging process. On OCLC coding became a part of cataloging done by the cataloger and, as such, was not timed separately.

The distribution of task frequencies remained fairly constant, again with the major exception of Task 2 which reflects the high number of contributed copies found in the OCLC data base. According to HSTS, "there was next to no contributed copy on RLIN." In spite of the increased burden on the copy-cataloger for tailoring of contributed card copy and coding for input, average times and costs were slightly lower on OCLC than on RLIN:

Table 9.   Copy-Cataloging Averages

	Average time per unit	Average cost per unit	Unit times		Unit costs	
			Lowest	Highest	Lowest	Highest
RLIN	8'50"	$1.32	3'	24'	$.45	$3.60
OCLC	8'33"	$1.28	4'	55'	$.60	$8.25

The wide range between the lowest and highest unit times and costs on OCLC gives an indication of the extra work which is occasionally required to recode and correct contributed copy on that system.

4.   Full Cataloging—Personnel Cost Summary and Comparison. Major differences between the two systems were those already found under copy-cataloging:

a.   Coding became part of the cataloger's workload on OCLC and, as such, was not timed separately.
b.   A large portion of contributed copy, even NLM copy, required corrections in either description or coding. HSTS estimated that corrections are much more time consuming than cataloging originals had been on RLIN.

Our sample distribution of task frequencies was the following:

Table 10. Cataloging Tasks

Task #	Task Description	% of Full Cataloging Task Frequency To Total Units	
		RLIN	OCLC
1	Descriptive cataloging	92	95
2	Classification work	53	35
3	Subject work	57	56
4	Name, Main, Added Entry Work	30	54
5	Change of entry	11	17
6	Coding	—	98

The decrease in descriptive cataloging and classification work indicates fewer "originals"; conversely, the increase in changes of entry, name, main and added entry work is due to more contributed copy on OCLC.

The impact of coding, recoding and corrections is visible also in average unit times and costs given below:

Table 11. Cataloging Averages

	Average time per unit	Average cost per unit	Unit times		Unit costs	
			Lowest	Highest	Lowest	Highest
RLIN	13'27"	$2.93	8'	24'	$1.76	$ 5.28
OCLC	14'15"	$3.13	4'	65'	$ .88	$14.30

Again, we found a wide range between the lowest and highest unit times and costs on OCLC, which supports HSL contention that dealing with contributed copy can be more time consuming than cataloging originals.

5. Post-cataloging—Personnel Cost Summary and Comparison. The advent of OCLC, and the CLSI circulation system within a short time contributed to several changes in post-cataloging activities, both in task content and sequence. Salient procedural changes and their effects were the following:

a. By producing serials and AV card sets, OCLC eliminated the need for "In House" card production and handling. Since similar developments have taken place on RLIN as well, the cost for "In House" card production under RLIN was excluded from consideration.

b. The typing of "subjects" on cards was eliminated on OCLC— tracings are included on shelf list only.

c. RLIN-produced cards were revised word for word by an LA III. On OCLC only additions and changes to the existing record are revised, and revision is done on-line before the cards are ordered. An LA III revises "changes" and an Associate Librarian revises "originals." Input records are kept in a "Save File" for 7 days, and revisions must take place before then. Upon receipt of the cards, an LA III briefly revises all sets. HSTS staff feels this method of revision provides better quality control.

d. Contributed copy may be updated in OCLC between the time of the original search and input. Given this chance, operators must compare corrections made by the cataloger to the updated record in the database and decide on the course of action to follow. This situation did not occur in RLIN due to the small incidence of contributed copy.

e. Book pockets, still used while on RLIN, were dropped because of the automated circulation control system, CLSI—a time saving. Without book pockets, security labels became trickier to place as paste renders the circuit ineffective—a time drain. OCLC provides computer produced spine labels and book tags—a time saving.

f. Coding was simpler on RLIN, although changes were being introduced at the time HSL was switching to OCLC.

On OCLC more fields need to be coded. Inputting time is longer also because each field must be sent and acknowledged separately, and each time a message is ready for transmission, the send signal is queued into messages from other OCLC users. Time required to input a record is therefore more dependent on the queuing mix and the processing time available at the OCLC central computer.

The changes described above would invalidate a task by task comparison, but by regrouping various task components we can compare the results:

Table 12. Cataloging Cost Breakdown

	RLIN Aver. Costs		OCLC Aver. Costs	
	Original	Copy	Original	Copy
Book processing	.57	.57	.45	.45
Book tags, labels			.23	.23
Card Preparation				
Code	.38	.15		
Input	1.05	.32	2.95	.60
Revision-manual	.42	.42		
-machine			.42	.30
Type subjects		.03		
Revise cards			.28	.28
Totals	2.42	1.49	4.33	1.86

As we have seen before, RLIN costs include coding, which was shifted to the cataloging process on OCLC: were we to subtract coding from RLIN figures, the discrepancy in costs would be even higher.

On-line revision was quicker than manual, as HSTS staff had anticipated:

Table 13. Revision

	RLIN Average	OCLC Average
Revision of "changes"	2'57"	2"
Revision of "originals"	2'47"	1'53'

This clear advantage of OCLC, however, is not reflected in cost figures for "originals" because the task has been shifted from an LA III on RLIN, to an Associate Librarian, thus annulling the cost saving.

B. *Staff Utilization Summary*

There are two aspects to this topic: one is the shift of a specific task from one level of personnel to another, which may or may not include a change in the time required for the task, the other is the change in the time required to do the task, at the same level of personnel. During the preceding analysis of cataloging functions, a few instances of task shifting to a higher or lower staff level were mentioned. Table 14 points out the tasks in which shifts were found and gives average times so that the magnitude of each shift may be viewed easily. Changes in times for the same staff level, which were discussed before in terms of costs, are examined here from a different perspective. The summary of total time by employee level shows the relative position of each class in both systems.

Table 14. Employee Levels

Staff Level	RLIN Total Time By Level	OCLC Total Time By Level
Clerk	1′14″	1′14″
LA I	22′21″	21′34″
LA II	4′ 2″	7′21″
LA III	26′ 5″	36′26″
Associate Librarian	13′27″	16′ 8″
Total Time	67′ 9″	82′43″

The LA III level has absorbed the bulk of the time increase, with smaller increases going to the Librarian and the LA II. The LA I is the only level which has experienced a lower average time spent on OCLC than on RLIN.

Table 15. Staff Utilization Summary

Function and Task	RLIN Average Time	Level	OCLC Average Time	Level
1. Pre-Order Search				
Terminal Search: all orders	36″	LA II		
Appr. plan			104″	LA I
G & E			112″	LA II
Firm			87″	LA III
Prepare print-out, slips: all orders	51″	LA II		
Appr. plan			94″	LA I
G & E			42″	LA II
Firm			60″	LA III
Revision of Searches	26″	LA III	37″	LA III
Receipt of piece	51″	LA I	66″	LA I
Additional searches	193″	LA I	500″	LA I
2. Pre-Cataloging Search				
All tasks	155″	LA II	287″	LA II
3. Copy Cataloging				
All tasks	530″	LA III		
All tasks plus coding			513″	LA III
4. Full Cataloging				
All tasks	807″	Assoc. Lib.		
All tasks plus coding			855″	Assoc. Lib.

Table 15 (Continued)

Function and Task	RLIN Average Time	RLIN Level	OCLC Average Time	OCLC Level
5. Post Cataloging				
Receipt of book	40″	LA I	74″	LA I
Prepare book tags	103″	LA I	127″	LA I
Book processing	74″	Clerk	74″	Clerk
Revision	77″	LA III	77″	LA III
"Originals": coding	150″	LA III		
input	420″	LA III	1179″	LA III
revision of cards	167″	LA III		
revision—on-line			113″	Assoc. Lib.
"In-House": card prep.	683″	LA I		
revision	28″	LA I		
"Copy": input	172″	LA I	329″	LA I
prepare, file	99″	LA I		
revision	167″	LA III	120″	LA III
Revision of card sets-all kinds			113″	LA III

Again, a word of caution: These figures are not to be regarded as real times. The time required to process an average title is lower on both systems. These figures aggregate all alternate steps and are presented in this form for comparison purposes only.

C. Cataloging Services

1. *Out-of-Pocket Costs.*—Given the complexity of the rate schedules and the number of variables to be considered for each installation, the best indications of local out-of-pocket costs are those constructed for the HSL Annual Reports by dividing total utilities costs by the number of titles processed during the same period:

Table 16. Out-of-Pocket Cost

	RLIN July 1978– June 1979	RLIN July 1979– Dec. 1979	OCLC Dec. 1979– June 1980
Net Cost per title	$1.76	$1.93	$2.18

The survey published in the November–December 1979 issue of *Library Technology Reports*, includes tables showing estimated costs per title cataloged under both utilities.[7] For a library cataloging 2,500 titles a

year (the number closest to the HSL workload) with roughly 10% originals, at 1979 rates, the OCLC cost per title is $2.11, quite close to the
HLS figure. The figures suggest there might be very little opportunity for
lowering OCLC costs by appreciable amounts. On RLIN, given the same
conditions, the survey reports a cost per title of $2.83, an amount con-
siderably higher than HSL expenses in the same period of time. It must be
remembered that, during this period, HSL was a "guest user" of the main
library installation, and it was not assessed some of the costs, such as
communications and terminal maintenance.

2. *Hit Rates.* The "hit rate" is a measure widely used to determine
the value of utilities' data bases, and is often defined as the number of
times a searched-for record is found. All expectations pointed to a higher
hit rate on OCLC and all statistics available thus far fully support the
claim. During the sampling for this study we collected the following
figures:

Table 17. Hit Rate

		Records Search	Hits	% of Hits
RLIN				
Pre-order Search	July 1979	169	98	58
Pre-cataloging Search	August 1979	135	32	24
OCLC				
Pre-order Search	May–June 1980	381	282	74
Pre-cataloging Search	July 1980	403	131	32

The pre-cataloging search hit rate is understandably much lower than the
pre-order search since it represents searches for records which were
either "no hit" or "contributed copy only" at the time of the first search.
The 32% hit rate on OCLC second searches, after a high rate on first
searches suggests that OCLC contributors do not set "originals" aside
waiting for someone else to catalog and input, but share their cataloging
on a timely basis.

A variable to be considered in the comparison of hit rates is, obviously,
the nature and age of the material being searched. At the beginning of this
study it was felt that the best comparison would be obtained by searching
both databases for the same books, at the same time. HSL conducted this
sampling between January and February 1980, both in Acquisitions for a
three-week period, and in Cataloging, on three different days in the same
three-week period. The results were the following:

Table 18. Hit rate: Side-by-Side Sample

	Records Searched	MARC copy	%	Contr. copy	%	Total	%
RLIN							
Acquisitions	169	83	48	4	2	87	51.5
Catalog	135	75	55	8	6	83	61.5
OCLC							
Acquisitions	169	82	48.5	51	30	133	78.7
Catalog	135	76	56	35	26	111	82

In this sample, cataloging searches were recorded as "first searches" and should not be compared to cataloging searches from the previous sample. Hit rates are higher than Acquisitions rates because books are that much "older" and copy has been added to both databases during processing time.

The searchers' conclusions were: (1) MARC copy found was identical on both data bases at the same time: both utilities must be loading MARC tapes quickly and on an identical schedule; (2) More than twice the contributed copy for Health Sciences material was available on OCLC.

IV. PROCESSING TIME LAG

One of the usual expectations of an automated cataloging system is that it will diminish the time required for processing. Since quick delivery of materials is one of HSL's primary goals, it was felt that a new system should contribute to shorten, or at least maintain, the existing processing time lag. The following method was designed to measure time lag.

RLIN

Trucks were sampled at the completion of the cataloging process, before proceeding to book processing and shelving. Various dates were recorded from the ORC for each title on the truck. The date of receipt of the material was shown on one multiple order slip. Time lapse was calculated in working days from the date of receipt to the cataloging date recorded on the ORC. Shelving date would have been preferable, but it was impossible to calculate at the time of the study.

One group of titles was consistently excluded: The Special Collection deferred cataloging, which is essentially special project materials. If we included those titles, the resulting distribution would have been skewed and would be misleading. A frequency distribution was constructed and plotted for the first sample. Five additional trucks were then sampled on a weekly basis to establish the reliability of the first sample. The six samples were pooled and results shown on a combined frequency distribution and graph on Tables 19 and 20. The figures were plotted at ten-day intervals, and the relative percentages were calculated.

Table 19. RLIN Processing Time Lag

Frequency Distribution

Days	#		Days	#	
1	2		38	3	
2	2		39	8	
3	1		40	1	
4	4		41	3	
5	3	15%	42	4	
6	1		43	1	
7	4		44	1	
8	8		45	2	
9	4		48	2	
10	7		52	1	
12	6		53	1	
13	3		54	2	
14	6		55	1	
15	2	16%	57	1	
16	3		58	1	20%
17	1		60	2	
18	2		62	2	
19	2		66	1	
20	2		68	2	
21	4		69	2	
22	4		74	1	
23	3		75	1	
24	2	17%	76	1	
25	5		81	1	
26	5		91	1	
27	5		105	1	
28	1		109	2	
29	2		122	1	
30	5		127	2	
31	4		129	1	
32	5		130	1	
33	3		131	2	7%
34	8	25%	134	1	
35	5		135	2	
36	5		143	1	
37	3		145	1	
			156	1	

Table 20. RLIN Processing Time Lag

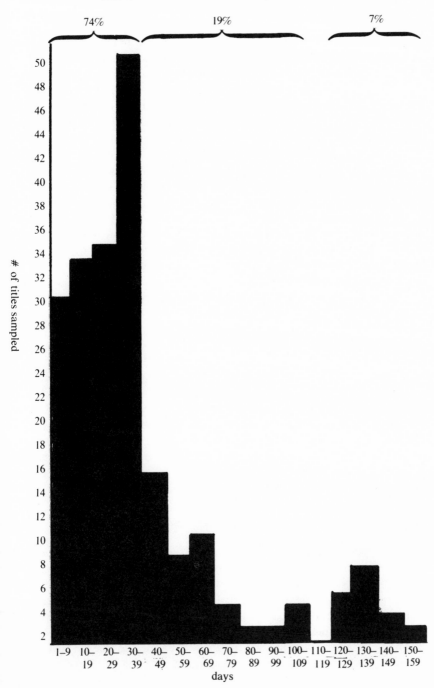

In examining the distribution, a reader should be aware of the following HSL policies:

1. Trade publications were to be held no longer than thirty days. If no copy was available by then, they were cataloged as originals.
2. Nontrade publications were to be held no longer than six months.

The titles sampled were 194. Included were all titles cataloged between Sept. 26 and Oct. 5, and between Nov. 7 and Dec. 7, 1979. To add context to the sample size, it should be said that the sample represented approximately 5% of all titles cataloged in one fiscal year (3,769 titles were cataloged by HSL in 1978–79).

In retrospect, this was not a good time to sample the cataloging time lag in HSTS because, (1) the pre-cataloging position was vacant during most of the sampling, and, (2) the two catalogers were busy much of the time with pressing matters of personnel interviewing and studying MARC formats in preparation for the OCLC switch. Nevertheless, the results are impressive: 74% of all titles sampled were cataloged within forty working days of receipt. See Table 20 for other breakdowns.

The next step was to break down the total processing time and separately calculate time spans for each title at each step, to show the relative magnitude of each process. The pie chart in Table 21 gives this breakdown. As expected the cataloging step consumed the longest time span.

OCLC

In order to obtain comparable figures on OCLC, it would have been necessary to wait until materials partially processed under RLIN had cleared all workstations. In addition, the HSL staff felt that it was much too soon to do a processing time lag study on OCLC and requested a postponement of the sampling to a later date. Consequently, no data was collected on the impact of OCLC on the time required for processing. That portion of the study will be performed later.

V. CONCLUSIONS

All data presented so far can be summarized in one sentence: except for copy-cataloging, each task took longer and was more expensive on OCLC than on RLIN. The consistency of the findings, across the whole OCLC processing operation, timed by at least ten employees over a period of five months, cannot be easily discarded as a statistical quirk or a peculiarity of the sample.

The first general conclusion arrived at by various sources in HSL is that the OCLC sampling was done too soon after the switch to the new system

Table 21. RLIN Processing Time Lag

% of Total Time Spent on Each Part of the Process

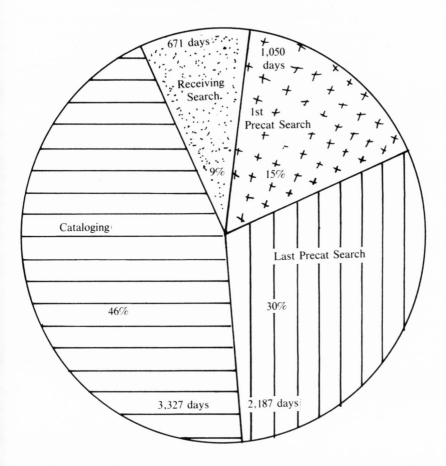

Cumulative working days for all titles in sample 7,235

From receipt of material to Receiving Search	671 cumulative days
From receiving Search to 1 st Precat Search	1,050 cumulative days
From 1st to Last Precat Search	2,187 cumulative days
From Last Precat Search to Catalog date	3,327 cumulative days

and, as such, that part of the study should be considered as "preliminary." HSL suggested, in their comments of November 1980, that
another sample be taken "later, after HSL has learned the new system."
There is some validity to this claim and some evidence to suggest that the

learning curve, indeed, had not yet flattened out, even at the time of the last sample taken. The evidence is as follows:

1. Procedures still used in May and June 1980, such as the printing and reporting of duplicate records to OCLC, were discovered to be unnecessary and later dropped.
2. The routine for displaying, inputting and printing spine labels was apparently revised and simplified after the sampling, in October 1980.
3. As of October 1980, enhancement functions which narrowed the search strategy became available, shortening search time and eliminating some dead-end searches, according to HSTS.
4. On pre-cataloging searches, contributed copy is no longer printed when found, but only at the end of the holding period, whether one month or six months.
5. As late as November 1980, searchers reported they were still gaining in speed, as their experience on the system increased. The same feeling was expressed by coders, with the exception of the Associate Librarian who did not feel the sample had been taken too soon. However, she is the person who had experienced the most in-depth, advance preparation, study, and training.
6. Of the pre-cataloging search tasks retimed on OCLC in October, one did not yield a lower unit time than the earlier sample: 18″ versus 34″.

We had anticipated a learning period and allowed a minimum of three months before we began timing on the new system, which became six months by the time we studied the last procedure. If another sampling, at a later date, were to confirm that people were still picking up speed six to nine months after the system became operational, the following implications should be considered in future experiments:

1. A learning period of three to six months is inadequate. When considering a switch in cataloging utilities, we should allow upwards of nine months before counting on the realization of significant gains;
2. The amount of negative transfer[8] has been underestimated up till now. The fact that all tasks took longer, even those small, purely manual ones which one would think not directly related to the utility in question, could be an indication of lingering negative transfer.

The second conclusion deals with staff utilization and is a corollary of the first. In his comparison of bibliographic utilities, Matthews states that

51% of libraries surveyed reported actual benefits in reassignment of staff and eliminated positions under OCLC[9]. Sixty-five % also reported a re-organization in technical services following OCLC installation. While the HSL experience differs in that the switch was from one utility to another, rather than from manual to automated, the reassignments of staff were mostly from lower to higher staff levels, and no major reorganization took place. It may well be argued that this upward shifting is a temporary phenomenon, again, a function of the unflattened learning curve, and that higher level staff is being assigned certain tasks simply because the per-sonnel is available. Once these tasks have been mastered, presumably they will be downshifted.

The third general conclusion is that the processing time lag appears to be shorter on OCLC. Books seem to be moving through Technical Ser-vices faster; analytics are now searched on receipt and those with copy cataloged immediately, rather than waiting six to eight months; searching backlog appears smaller; cards are received sooner; the delay in obtaining and filing cards sets for serials and AV's has diminished from three and one-half months to three to four weeks. Some of these improvements, such as serials cards production, might well have occurred under RLIN also. Given HSL's stated goal of providing quick delivery of material to its patrons, this topic deserves further study.

More specifically it was found that searching takes longer on OCLC and corporate name searching is particularly time consuming. More copy is found on OCLC, but some ambivalent feeling exists as to the quality of this copy. Early in the life of the system HSL stated that OCLC copy was "excellent." This euphoria subsided somewhat after a few months of experience on the whole system, and comments received in November 1980 indicated that dealing with OCLC copy "slows down work" as it often must be recoded; even NLM copy was often incomplete and fol-lowed different standards; on-line maintenance and corrections were time consuming and complicated. The statement was made that originals on RLIN were "easier and faster to prepare by cataloger than making cor-rections on OCLC contributed copy." Our sample statistics were aggre-gates and did not lend themselves to this breakdown. Assuming that statement to be true, however, a library would want to minimize the use of marginal copy (the greatest advantage of OCLC) and the waiting period between first search and final input. Finding the precise breaking point in time between the chance of losing more MARC copy and that of obtaining more contributed copy is more of an art than a science. HSTS was very sensitive to changes in this area and is constantly evaluating the benefits of additional "holds" periods against the returns, adjusting its procedures accordingly.

The next set of conclusions revolve around technical factors, all beyond local control. All HSL findings are congruent with those reported in the Matthews survey.

1. Down time appeared better on OCLC, with slightly less loss of inputting time.
2. Response time was somewhat slower on OCLC.
3. Better cooperation was received from OCLC on complaints and requests. Complaints and letters were often not answered by RLIN for many weeks.
4. Direct costs are quite similar.
5. Turnaround time in card receipt is about equal, with a slight OCLC advantage.
6. MARC tapes are loaded on identical schedules.

Advantages and disadvantages in this area tend to balance each other out so that neither system emerges with clear superiority.

There were some additional OCLC advantages cited at various times by HSL staff: being able to keep inputting up to date; smaller backlog; less need for batching; no need to travel to the main library, and avoidance of long delays if that system or communication lines were down. While these elements are all beneficial, at least psychologically, they were not pursued in detail as they seemed to be advantages which are inherent in having in-house terminals and longer terminal hours, rather than being advantages of the OCLC system. Finally, there was no evidence in any of the Technical Processing areas to suggest that HSL has had to relax its high standards to accommodate the new system.

NOTES

1. *Librarian's Handbook for Costing Network Services* (Boulder: Western Interstate Library Coordinating Organization and Western Interstate Commission for Higher Education, 20 December, 1976), p. 20.

2. Betty Jo Mitchell, Norman E. Tanis, and Jack Jaffe, *Cost Analysis of Library Functions: A Total Systems Approach* (Greenwich: Jay Press, 1978), pp. 15–34.

3. *Librarian's Handbook*, p. 10.

4. Ibid., pp. 11–12.

5. Ibid., pp. 20–21.

6. Robert M. Hayes and Joseph Becker, *Handbook of Data Processing for Libraries*, 2nd ed. (New York: Wiley, 1974), p. 120.

7. Joseph R. Matthews, "The Four Online Bibliographic Utilities: A Comparison," *Library Technology Reports*, v. 15, no. 6 (Chicago: American Library Association, 1979), pp. 746–753.

8. Negative transfer is the interference of past skills and activities in learning and new skills or applications which are similar enough to be confusing. Applies to motor activities as well as "mind set".

9. *The Four Online Bibliographic Utilities*, pp. 754–756.

A COMPARISON OF RLIN AND OCLC: HIT RATE, QUALITY OF MEMBER COPY, AND CODING

Diana Gray

This paper will analyze the results of a side-by-side study of the Research Libraries Group's Research Library Information Network (RLIN) and the OCLC technical processing system at the Peter J. Shields Library, University of California, Davis. The purpose of the study was to determine the significance of the differences between the systems, if such existed, in regard to the hit rate and response time and the quality of cataloging. In addition, an attempt was made to determine if member copy in either system was sufficiently reliable in quality and consistency of cataloging practice to be handled by the nonprofessional copy-cataloging staff at Davis. A basic criterion, therefore, was the inclusion of the LC Classification Number (LCCN) and LC Subject Headings (LCSH), since records using non-LC classification or subject headings are always handled by professional catalogers at Davis. The evaluation was to be informal, not a scientific study in which statistical analyses were to be employed. The intellectual skills required to compare records were those used when comparing copy during the cataloging process. The data was collected between October and November 1980.

HIT RATE AND RESPONSE TIME

There were three categories employed in the searching process: Foreign and Domestic Pre-Order, Approval Plan receipts, and "Hold-for-Copy." The latter category refers to titles, both firm order and Approval Plan books, which had been held for up to six months after receipt since no copy had been located in earlier searches of RLIN. Between October and November 1,736 titles were searched. Only monographs and analytics were searched; serials, scores, and other nonbook formats were excluded from the test group. The study revealed that the overall hit rate in OCLC ran to 68%, and in RLIN, 50%. The hit rate for Foreign Pre-Order searches, however, was 10% higher in RLIN, but overall, no appreciable differences in Pre-Order search results were discovered. For the Approval Plan and Hold-for-Copy categories, OCLC's hit rates were considerably higher than RLIN, 30% and 35%, respectively (Table 22). The individual hits were then broken down into two categories: MARC and member contributed copy. Generally, there were a greater number of full MARC (FMRC) and fewer cataloging in publication (CIP) records in OCLC than in RLIN (Table 23). A significantly higher percentage of member copy was found in OCLC for Approval Plan and Hold-for-Copy items, but the reverse was true for Pre-order materials—RLIN higher, but to a lesser degree (Table 24).

Table 22. Hit Rate

	No. Titles	*RLIN*			*OCLC*		
		Min.	Hits	% Hits	Min.	Hits	% Hits
Pre-Order Foreign	413	399	254	62%	412	213	52%
Domestic	359	320	223	62%	326	255	71%
A. Total Pre-Order	772	719	477	62%	738	468	61%
B. Approval	414	500	172	42%	458	297	72%
C. Hold-for-Copy	550	415	219	40%	478	410	75%
Total A, B, C	1736	1634	868	50%	1674	1175	68%

Overall Hit Rate $\frac{868}{1736} = 50\%$ Overall Hit Rate $\frac{1175}{1736} = 68\%$

Table 23. MARC Records

		RLIN		*OCLC*	
		No.	%	No.	%
A.	Pre-Order Foreign				
	FMRC	142	91%	149	93%
	CIP	14	9%	12	7%
	TOTAL	156	100%	161	100%
	Pre-Order Domestic				
	FMRC	81	44%	100	54%
	CIP	102	56%	84	46%
	TOTAL	183	100%	184	100%
	Total Pre-Order:				
	FMRC	223	66%	249	72%
	CIP	116	34%	96	28%
	TOTAL	339	100%	345	100%
B.	Approval				
	FMRC	47	31%	70	46%
	CIP	103	69%	83	54%
	TOTAL	150	100%	153	100%
C.	Hold-for-Copy				
	FMRC	126	99%	143	99%
	CIP	1	1%	1	1%
	TOTAL	127	100%	144	100%

Table 24. MARC/Member Ratio

		RLIN		OCLC	
		No.	%	No.	%
A.	Pre-Order Foreign				
	MARC*	156	61%	161	76%
	member	98	39%	52	24%
	TOTAL	254	100%	213	100%
	Pre-Order Domestic				
	MARC	183	82%	184	72%
	member	40	18%	71	28%
	TOTAL	223	100%	255	100%
	Total Pre-Order:				
	MARC	339	71%	345	74%
	member	138	29%	123	26%
	TOTAL	477	100%	468	100%
B.	Approval				
	MARC	150	87%	153	52%
	member	22	13%	144	48%
	TOTAL	172	100%	297	100%
C.	Hold-for-Copy				
	MARC	127	58%	144	35%
	member	92	42%	266	65%
	TOTAL	219	100%	410	100%

*Includes full MARC and CIP records.

Response time, or the rate of searching time per title, was nearly the same in both systems, both under 1 minute per title.

Table 25. Search Time in Minutes

	RLIN		OCLC	
	Average Per Title	Total	Average Per Title	Total
Pre-Order	.93	719	.96	738
Approval	1.21	500	1.09	458
Hold-for-Copy	.75	415	.87	478
		1634 min.		1674 min.

Total Time $\dfrac{1634\ \text{min.}}{1736\ \text{titles}} = .94$ min. $\dfrac{1674\ \text{min.}}{1736\ \text{titles}} = .96$ min.

On the other hand, in terms of time required to produce a successful hit, OCLC yielded a better result because of OCLC's decidedly superior hit rate (Table 26).

Table 26. Minutes per Hit

	RLIN	OCLC
Pre-Order	1.51	1.58
Approval	2.91	1.54
Hold-for-Copy	1.89	1.17
Total Time $\frac{1634 \text{ min.}}{868 \text{ hits}} = 1.88$		$\frac{1674 \text{ min.}}{1775 \text{ hits}} = 1.42$

Conclusion

The overall hit rate in OCLC was 18% higher than in RLIN: 68%–50%. Although RLIN did have a higher hit rate for Pre-Order title searches, 62%–61%, OCLC yielded a significantly higher hit rate in the remaining two categories, in the range of 30% to 35%. There was no significant difference in response time, or rate of searching time per title, but it took less time to locate a hit in OCLC than in RLIN because of the higher hit rate.

OCLC showed a higher number of full MARC records retrieved per category and fewer CIP records than in RLIN. CIP records appear to be replaced in OCLC by full MARC records more quickly than in RLIN. RLIN had a higher proportion of member copy for Pre-Order titles, 29%–26%, but the highest proportion of member copy was in OCLC for Approval Plan: 48%–13%, and Hold-for-Copy: 65%–42%.

The higher hit rate in OCLC is a function of the database size as well as the number of participants. There are 2,200 cataloging agencies in OCLC, 143 in RLIN. At the time of the study, only 36 libraries of 15 RLG institutions were using RLIN for cataloging. In addition, OCLC has more data files available at present: National Library of Medicine (NLM), National Agricultural Library (NAL), Government Printing Office (GPO), and the 1968–72 MARC tapes. RLIN, on the other hand, has already scheduled for 1981/82 the loading of the 1968–72 MARC tapes and former OCLC users' archives files, and plans to acquire tapes from NAL, NLM, and GPO are proceeding apace. When all scheduled tapes are loaded and when all RLG libraries are active cataloging participants, it is expected that the size of the database and corresponding hit rates will be greater. Therefore, it should be kept in mind that RLIN's hit rates indicated in this study are not stable and are subject to fluctuation as each RLG member starts active participation in cataloging and each file is loaded into RLIN.

QUALITY COMPARISON
In this study we established five criteria which had to be met for a member record to be considered suitable for nonprofessional treatment. The first two were objective standards that reflected contributors' local cataloging policy. The last three dealt with the completeness and quality of the records, which reflect Davis's cataloging standards and policy. Evaluation of these records involved, to a greater or lesser degree, subjective judgment of the evaluator. All the criteria had to be satisfied for a record to be considered acceptable (Table 27). To calculate the total number of unacceptable records, an analysis was made of each of the five criteria, and a deficiency in any one would render that record unacceptable. For example, if a record met criteria A through D but failed E, it was considered unacceptable. What we sought were "perfect" records in our eyes which could be easily processed without professional intervention. In our practice at Davis, copy-catalogers may bibliographically describe a book and may also enhance descriptive cataloging found in a copy, but they are not permitted to assign classification, subject headings, judge the adequacy of subject headings, or determine choice and form of access points. The criteria used were:

A. LC classification (LCCN)
B. LC Subject Headings (LCSH)
C. Appropriate and Specific Subject Headings
D. LC-Authorized Choice and Form of Names
E. Bibliographic Description

Also examined was the coding of the fixed and variable fields of the MARC format (Table 33). The attempt here was simply to determine whether there was an appreciable difference in the level of coding and, if there was a difference, what impact it might have for the users of the systems. The study compared cataloging copy only; copy was not compared with the book. The LC classification number was not examined for correctness; the fact that it was present in the record made it eligible for acceptability. The study included member copy only. While MARC records and the in-process-file (IPF) records from Stanford University were counted as hits in Table 22, they were excluded from the study of quality.

Of the 1,736 titles searched there were 166 matches of OCLC and RLIN member copy. Twenty-six titles had IPF records and were not included in the evaluation. This left 140 member titles for actual comparison. Since all the member copies are available on-line to users of the RLIN, we included 31 RLIN records which yielded 49 multiple records. In all, 189 RLIN records for 140 titles were examined. In order to determine which record was more complete as in E. Bibliographic Description, or which record used more extensive subject analysis, as in Table 31: More Specific Subject Heading Analysis, each OCLC record was compared with each RLIN copy, including the multiple hits. If, for example, an OCLC record were more complete than any of RLIN's four records for that title, that OCLC record was credited four records as being more complete.

Table 27. Records Accepted

RLIN			OCLC		
No. Records	Accept.	%	Records	Accept.	%
189	111*	59%	140	70	50%

*102 of these were contributed by RLG libraries (92%)

Table 28 illustrates the five categories of criteria and the number of records which had deficiencies in each of these areas. Each category was evaluated separately. It should be noted that a record could have more than one deficient area, but one deficiency in any of the five categories was sufficient to make a record unacceptable.

Table 28. Criteria

	RLIN			OCLC		
	No. Records	Not Accept.	%	No. Records	Not Accept.	%
A. *LCCN*	189	43	23%	140	37	26%
B. *LCSH*	189	14	7%	140	10	7%
C. *SH Choice*	189	8	4%	140	16	11%
D. *LC Authorized Names*	34	16	47%	34	13	38%
E. *Bibl. Desc.*	189	33	17%	189	52	28%

A–B.   LCCN and LCSH

A higher percentage of OCLC records did not use the LCCN: 20% as against 23% for RLIN, yet 7% did not use LC subject headings in both systems. NAL and NLM records found in OCLC used the non-LCSH exclusively. Ten records used the NAL and NLM classifications in OCLC, and the remaining 27 used either Dewey or no classification at all. Forty-three RLIN records in this category used either Dewey or no classification. The users of Dewey were primarily art libraries which tended also to be users of subject heading schemes other than LCSH.

Conclusion

There was no significant difference in the percentage of records in either system considered unacceptable because of the absence of the LC classification and subject heading systems.

C. *Subject Heading Choice*

Precisely because this category, as well as the next two, required some subjective analysis involved in the determination of bibliographic completeness and quality, it was felt to be important to create objectively verifiable criteria to minimize the risk of individual preference prevailing in judgment. Consequently, a subject heading was considered inadequate or inappropriate if it:

1. Was too general, e.g., "Reading" alone was used, when the subtitle stated ". . . comprehensive exercises for secondary public school use." The heading, "Reading (Secondary education)— Handbooks, manuals, etc." would have been more appropriate than the single "Reading."
2. Did not correspond with the LC Classification, e.g., "English literature," was required when the book was classed in PR, instead of "Literature."
3. Incorrectly used indirect geographical subdivisions, e.g., "Canada . . . Ontario."
4. Transposed the main heading and its subdivisions, e.g., "Emigration—Spain."
5. Incorrectly spelled geographic subdivisions.
6. Contained no subject headings at all, when the subject matter required them.
7. Omitted necessary subdivisions, e.g., "Criticism and interpretation."

Subject headings reflecting possible local practice were not considered: for example, in cataloging an art exhibit catalog, Davis, which has a divided catalog, requires the artist's name as a subject heading, even when the main entry is the artist also.

Examination showed that the RLIN records on the whole had more subject headings per record than the OCLC records, and a large percentage of them were LC Subject Headings (Tables 29–30). RLIN records also used more specific LC subject treatment (more subdivisions, chronological breakdowns, etc.) than did the OCLC records (Table 31).

Table 29.　Average Subject Headings per Record

RLIN		OCLC	
Total Records	Average	Total Records	Average
189	2.03	140	1.93

Table 30.　Average LCSH per Record

RLIN		OCLC	
Total Records	Average	Total Records	Average
189	1.80	140	1.70

Table 31.　More Specific LCSH Analysis

RLIN			OCLC		
Total Records Compared	No.	%	Total Records Compared	No.	%
189	52*	28%	189	35	19%

*44 of the 52 were contributed by RLG libraries (85%)

Noting that 85% of the headings with more specific subject analysis were contributed by RLG libraries, one may posit that research libraries tend to require more specific subject headings. One may surmise that the situation obtains in research libraries participating in OCLC as well, but since the OCLC database record selects the "first in" as the base record (unless replaced by LC MARC), a strong element of research library cataloging was not reflected in sample records drawn for the study. It should be understood that the study of specificity is quite separate from the figures which appear in Table 28, C. The reasons for nonacceptance in these instances were inappropriateness and incorrectness of headings used.

Conclusion

RLIN records used slightly more LCSH per title than OCLC records. More impressive was the higher percentage of incidents in which RLIN records used more extensive subject analysis, and 85% of those were produced by RLG libraries.

D. LC Authorized Names

Although choice and form of LC authorized names were difficult to ascertain without book in hand, there were discrepancies that were noticed by comparing copy alone. (AACR2 headings were not available in OCLC during this study.) When a discrepancy arose, names were verified in the 1972–80 NUC Catalogs and in the data bases for MARC verification. As with Section E, Table 28, each OCLC record was compared against each RLIN record, including the multiples. Table 32 illustrates a breakdown of LC-authorized names discovered by discrepancies in the records. The names which were not verified are listed as undetermined.

Table 32. LC Authorized Names

	RLIN		OCLC	
	Total Records	%	Total Records	%
	34*	100%	34	100%
Acceptable	13	38%	16	47%
Not Acceptable	16	47%	13	38%
Undetermined	5	15%	5	15%

*Includes 25 titles with 9 multiples.

Not considered as a discrepancy were records that used title main entry instead of corporate or personal name, as long as all names were covered in the record. Some records could not be verified at all because the entries were too recent for verification and were the result of cataloging libraries simultaneously establishing a name for the first time. These were considered as undetermined. All of the 13 unacceptable records from OCLC were marked "Level I (Full Cataloging)." On the other hand, 6 unacceptable records from RLIN (37.5%) were marked Standard, the remaining 10 (62.5%) were tagged as non-Standard. While there were more incidents of non-LC authorized names in RLIN, nearly two-thirds of those clearly carried the warning that these records may require further work. The non-Standard designation in RLIN thus alerts the user that the record does not meet the RLIN requirements for Standard cataloging.

As expected, most of the multiple records in RLIN were built on existing records which, in turn, increased the percentage of non-LC authorized names. Users apparently found a record in RLIN and used that record as their authority without checking further. This short cut is in theory a sound procedure; it is economical of staff time and speeds processing time. However, when an original record is not updated or verified against the latest LC authority, there is a danger that the wrong heading is multiplied and perpetuated. Because OCLC has only one database record visible to the user, the multiplying effect of incorrect headings in the database record being copied by other libraries cannot be measured.

The situation leads to the speculation that the higher incidence of current LC authorized names in OCLC may result from the fact that a successful retrieval is contingent on exact word order. In other words, if a cataloger employed a correct LC version of a name and used the exact word order in that name for retrieval, only records with the correct name would be retrieved; at the same time, entering a wrong form of name would retrieve no record whatever. In RLIN, however, the key word-searching strategy prints all records with those key words, regardless of order, to be retrieved. Had the very desirable capability of key word search been available in OCLC, variant records, in this case incorrect, would probably have been retrieved. For instance, in the following example, only by searching under the LC heading can this record be retrieved in OCLC:

Workshop of the United States/Australia Rangelands Panel, 3rd, Tucson, Ariz., 1973.

In RLIN the key words, "rangelands panel," will retrieve both the LC authorized form and other forms:

United States/Australia Rangelands Panel Workshop, 3rd, Tucson, Ariz., 1973.
Workshop of the United States/Australia Rangelands Panel, 3rd, Tucson, Ariz., 1973.

To illustrate further, in OCLC the LC-authorized form of corporate name must be constructed properly, since retrieval begins with the first word which is not a stop word:

Joint FAO/IAEA/WHO Advisory Group on International Acceptance of Irradiated Food

In RLIN the key words, "joint irradiated," will retrieve:

International acceptance of irradiated food (title main entry)
Joint FAO/IAEA/WHO Advisory Group on International Acceptance of Irradiated Food

In both cases the RLIN user can locate the records with the significant key words. This situation seems to indicate that under certain conditions, RLIN users should be more careful in selecting what appears to be an authoritative heading. Of course, records can be successfully retrieved in both systems by title searches or by combined name/title searches.

Conclusion

OCLC had a higher percentage of LC authorized names: 47% to 38%. Ten records in RLIN using non-LC authorized names were tagged as "non-Standard" records. All the problem records in OCLC were tagged "Level I (Full Cataloging)." Thus non-Standard tagging in RLIN records appears to be a fairly reliable indication of less than full cataloging treatment, while OCLC's "Level I" does not appear to be a reliable indication of full cataloging because both adequate and inadequate records carry that tag.

E. Bibliographic Description

Records were compared against each other as in Table 28, D. Incompletely described records included:

1. Incomplete 260≠a and b (place and publisher), especially if there were double imprints.
2. Missing bibliography and index notes.
3. Missing 245≠c (author statement) with the record coded as author present.
4. 245≠c personal author, not editor, for a title main entry.
5. Missing 250 (edition statement).
6. Incorrect placement for edition statement (most often apeared in the title field).
7. Leaves described as pages or vice versa (not incorrect if the calculation in each description was equivalent, e.g., 16 pages, 32 leaves.
8. Missing desirable information, such as notes describing language of text and summaries, bibliographic history and so forth.

Not considered in this evaluation were preliminary paging, ISBD punctuation, absence of contents notes, or possible local practice decisions, such as added entries for publishers or authors of prefaces and other introductory material. Table 33 shows the total number of problems, by descriptive element found in the records. This table differs from Table 28, E., which showed the number of records rejected because of one or more missing elements in description. In all, there were 189 comparisons on 140 titles.

Table 33.   Incomplete Bibliographic Description

	Descriptive Element	RLIN Problems	OCLC Problems
1.	Place, Publisher	5	15
2.	Date	2	1
3.	Bibl. Note	6	13
4.	Subtitle	0	1
5.	Author	1	8
6.	Edition	5	7
7.	Pagination	7	5
8.	Illustration	12	8
9.	General Notes	14	20
10.	Index Note	2	19
11.	Added Entries	1	2
12.	LCCN	1	1
13.	ISBN	2	2
	TOTAL	58	102

Conclusion

The RLIN records had more complete bibliographic description. On the whole, RLIN included more notes describing language of texts and summaries, bibliographic histories, bibliographies and indexes, and correct formating of author statements. Forty-one records in RLIN which were found to be more bibliographically complete than in OCLC were contributed by RLG libraries. The OCLC records tended to use a more complete 300≠b (illustration statement) than did the RLIN records and were coded accurately. The most frequent omission in OCLC records were the bibliography and index notes.

Coding of Fixed and Variable Fields

Coding was not part of the criteria in Table 28, but it was considered along with the other criteria to determine the overall quality of records studied. In this section of the study the degree of completeness in bibliographic coding in member copy was assessed. A record that contained more than one coding error or omission was counted only once. For example, omission of coding would be declared for a record in which notes describing indexes and bibliographies were present, but no corresponding codes appeared in the fixed field, or vice-versa. If, however, the description agreed with the coding, the record was considered adequate, even if the matching record in the alternate system had additional codes and notes.

Table 34 shows that 50% of the OCLC records had missing or incomplete coding:

Table 34.   Incomplete Coding

RLIN			OCLC		
Total Records	*No.*	*%*	*Total Records*	*No.*	*%*
189	41	22%	140	70	50%

Of all the incomplete OCLC records, 5 (7%) were "Level I" records with no fixed field coding at all, while 7 RLIN records (17%) had no fixed field coding but were tagged as "non-Standard." Again the "non-Standard" tagging RLIN proved a fairly reliable indication of less adequate treatment.

Most of the coding errors in OCLC were the omission of the 041 (languages) and 043 (geographic area) codes. Others were inaccurate illustration and contents codes and in the fields where the system provided default values. These include Cataloging Source, Conference Publication, Country of Publication, Date Type, Index, and so forth. OCLC inserts default values in the fixed field portion of the workform for original cataloging. In many cases they appear to be left untouched by the cataloging agencies supplying the database record. RLIN does not employ default values and puts the burden of coding on the cataloging agencies themselves. The RLIN 1978 standards require that a record must be fully and completely coded to be considered "Standard." Although the December 1980 *Bibliographic Input Standards*[2] in OCLC require more mandatory codes for "Level I" records than the 1977 standards,[3] OCLC does not require correction of the default fields. Until the standards require rigorous coding, retrieval by fixed fields will not be possible in OCLC as it will be in RLIN. Retrieval by fixed fields simply means formulating a search strategy from the codes in the record, such as languages, country of publication, type of document, format, range of imprint years, geographic area covered, and so forth. This capability has special significance for research libraries, whose patrons will need this kind of in-depth exploitation of information contained in the database.

Two undesirable consequences are the results of incomplete coding in the database record. The first is the production of incomplete records for participating members, and the second, that it requires additional effort at the local cataloging agency to supply the deficient coding. To add to the negative aspects of incomplete original coding, local additions are not available to members who may use the database record at a later date.

Summary

As expected, OCLC demonstrated its unquestioned superiority in hit rate. Because hits occurred more frequently in OCLC, searching for bibliographic records appears to be appreciably more efficient in OCLC than on RLIN, although the time required to search an item was quite similar in the two systems. In our evaluation of member copy, we found that more of OCLC's records contained current LC authorized names than did the RLIN records. We found that exactly the same proportion of copies used LC Subject Headings, but in all the remaining categories, the RLIN sample contained more acceptable records than the OCLC sample. RLIN copies had more subject heading, more extensive subject analysis, and more complete bibliographic description and coding. Most of the copies found in RLIN were from research institutions. More significantly, we found that records from the libraries of the Research Library Group have made a decided impact on the quality and thoroughness of RLIN member copy. Specifically we discovered that of the RLIN acceptable records, the following was the situtation:

85% of the subject headings with more extensive analysis were produced by RLG libraries (Table 31)
79% of the records that contained more complete bibliographic description were from RLG libraries (from Table 28)
82% of the more completely coded records were RLG records (from Table 34)
92% of all the acceptable records were from RLG institutions (Table 27)

Having examined in detail copies obtained from the two systems, we can say that the advantage of a high hit rate appears to be negated to a degree by the less reliable quality of member copy found in OCLC. Therefore, it is incorrect to assume that a higher hit rate translates into a more efficient system.

Applying the results of the study to our own cataloging environment, we may draw certain conclusions. At Davis, the copy-cataloging unit of the Catalog Department is staffed predominantly by Library Assistants II who process LC MARC and RLG member copies obtained from RLIN. They verify and make minor modification to descriptive cataloging, may add certain types of notes, for example, index and bibliography notes, and supply coding where needed. Library Assistants III and IV are given catalog copies produced by RLIN members who are not RLG members. Library Assistants are asked to bring to the attention of the Principal Cataloger any copy that appears to have problems which are beyond their prescribed level of responsibility. These problems might include suspicious subject headings, choice and form of name entries, and complex bibliographic problems.

Besides original cataloging, professional catalogers are given problem RLIN copies, most of which lack LC call numbers and/or LC Subject Headings. Using the above method of distribution, we have maintained an 85%–15% proportion between nonprofessional and professional cataloging. Our findings lead us to believe that we would be required to employ a larger percentage of professional catalogers if we were to use OCLC for cataloging.

The job of distribution of RLIN copy, performed by a Library Assistant II, is not a difficult or time-consuming operation because of several features unique to RLIN. First, the cataloging practice followed by RLG member libraries is similar to the practice at Davis and the quality of their cataloging is high and consistent. Those RLG members who follow dissimilar practices are primarily specialized libraries, such as art, law, and music, and are easily recognizable. Also, the tagging on RLIN records is a reliable indication that the record either represents the most complete cataloging, or it does not. If not, the record is sent automatically to a cataloger, eliminating the need for an intervening professional decision.

If we were to use OCLC copy for cataloging at the nonprofessional level, it would require copy-catalogers to pay far more rigorous attention to coding (28% more than RLIN) and bibliographic description (11% more than RLIN). Davis policy states that expert subject analysis and choice and form of access points require professional attention. Therefore, these two factors take on significance in terms of quality evaluation and efficient staff utilization. In addition, our policy regards subject analysis as an activity that should not be handled by copy-catalogers. Consequently, the risk inherent in the nonprofessional processing of OCLC copy with inferior subject analysis would force us to replace our nonprofessional with professional catalogers were we to move to OCLC. In academic and research libraries with large subject files, such as Davis, using OCLC records would represent some risk of separating catalog records for books that treat the same or similar subject contents. Our study showed the subject analysis provided by RLG institutions met our requirements and was comparable to the analysis produced by our professional cataloging staff. The need for care regarding current LC authorized names is recognized, but careful searching routines conscientiously followed will avoid most potential name conflicts before cataloging. Finally, the authority control subsystem which is scheduled for implementation in the summer of 1981 should provide a convenient method for identifying correct and incorrect names, and help to produce quality records that can be shared freely.

As mentioned earlier, all member records can be seen by users of RLIN. The ability to view all local records actually saves time for users because they can choose the most complete record. At the same time, we suspect that the inability of OCLC users to see more than a single database record and the further inability of the system to retain and display improved versions of the database record must constitute a sizeable loss of processing time for OCLC users as a whole.

Although it was stated that coding was considered to be more suitable for a clerical operation level than for a professional task, we do not denigrate its importance. In fact, we are convinced that as the database size increases, the importance of search strategies which employ the coded information as qualifiers will become even. Unless the current state of coding in OCLC is improved, retrieval using coded information will not net desired material in an efficient manner.

Both database systems provide what they characterize as high quality, full cataloging categories: "Standard" in RLIN and "Level I" in OCLC. It is absolutely requisite that these criteria be maintained so that users can correctly assume that records bearing the highest standard designation actually contain the fullest and most complete cataloging. RLG member records cataloged to "Standard" appear to merit such confidence. However, we found that OCLC's "Level I" records as a whole contained more variations than did RLIN's "Standard" records; therefore, we must conclude that the "Level I" designation as an indicator of full and complete cataloging is not very reliable. Furthermore, we found that many OCLC "Level I" records were deficient in coding and description, as well as in subject analysis. Under these circumstances, we would not be comfortable in entrusting the distribution of cataloging work to a Library Assistant II, as is now done. Whether or not the December 1980 *Bibliographic Input Standards* of OCLC will encourage and eventually raise the quality of member records and improve the predictability of their quality remains to be seen.

REFERENCES

1. "BALLOTS Standard for Cataloging Books" (unpublished document, BALLOTS Center, Stanford University, April 15, 1978), p. 2.

2. OCLC, Inc., *Bibliographic Input Standards, 1980 December.* (Columbus, Ohio: OCLC, Inc., c1980).
3. Ohio College Library Center, *Level I and Level K Input Standards, 1977 November,* (Columbus, Ohio, Ohio College Library Center, 1977).
4. "RLIN Standards for Cataloging and Content Designation" (unpublished document, Research Libraries Information Network, Inc., February 4, 1980).
5. "BALLOTS Standard for Cataloging Books."

GENERAL CONCLUSION

Kazuko M. Dailey

Comparing the results of the two studies, one finds a number of common threads. The indisputable advantage of OCLC is clearly its large and rich database. Furthermore, that advantage seems to lengthen over RLIN with time, because participating libraries contribute their original cataloging in a timely manner. This situation was reflected in both studies by the significantly larger number of hits in OCLC at every searching step after the receipt of books. The only exception noted was the availability of foreign titles in RLIN, which reflects the nature of research collections.

Incomplete coding found in OCLC member copies was another common finding. In the case of the Health Sciences Library, upgrading of coding became an add-on to the cataloger's work. Both studies found that the quality of OCLC member copy was somewhat more uneven than RLIN's. In the Jaroff study, the situation was reflected by the wide swing between the minimum and maximum times required for processing copies: OCLC's figures were 4 to 55 minutes as against RLIN's 3 to 24 minutes. Jaroff reported that 50% of OCLC's MARC fields required modification, while Gray reported 50% of OCLC's member copy was not acceptable for copy-cataloging. On examining the member copies in detail, Gray found that a larger number of OCLC copies did not meet the level of Davis cataloging standards, while a very large number of RLG member copies demonstrated consistently high quality.

It was somewhat surprising to find in Jaroff's study that in all accounts, except copy-cataloging, OCLC required more time, therefore larger staff costs, than did RLIN. Since the charges levied by OCLC and RLIN are quite similar, it appears that the Health Sciences Library's total cataloging cost is higher with OCLC than it was with RLIN. As Jaroff points out, six months may not be a sufficient period for adjustment from RLIN to OCLC, and we may experience some staff cost reduction in the future. It should be remembered, however, that staff costs incurred because of the system design, such as field-by-field mode of transmission required in OCLC, will not be affected by improving internal procedures.

Another unexpected result of the Jaroff study was the upward shift of task assignment. Whether it is a temporary aberration, resulting from an increased difficulty or complexity of using OCLC is not yet clear and requires further attention.

One felicitous result of using OCLC has been the apparent shortening of the time required for processing, that is, the time it takes to prepare a new book in for shelving in the stacks. From visual observation only, the Health Sciences staff believes that books are moving out of processing area more quickly and that many fewer books are held in the area waiting to be rechecked in the database for copy. Since the speed of processing is an important element of the total medical library service capability, any increase in processing costs which resulted from using OCLC should be weighed against the benefit of the early availability of the book to the patron. At the same time, efforts should be continued to find ways to reduce the time required for OCLC operation.

As for the Main Library, the findings of the Gray study lead us to conclude that RLIN, on the whole, is more suitable for cataloging operations of this research library than OCLC is likely to prove. The first problem we would encounter, if we were to adopt OCLC today, would be the reduced level of predictability and consistency of the quality of member copies found in the database. This deficiency, combined with the absence of a reliable indicator in the record, which would automatically calibrate the quality of copy, would mean that a person with a fairly sophisticated understanding of cataloging, probably a professional cataloger, would be assigned to examine all member copy to decide what level of cataloging expertise is required to process the piece. In our current RLIN operation, a Library Assistant II distributes the work, and we find this arrangement quite satisfactory. The reason which enables us to utilize a relatively low level employee for the task is inherent in the character of RLIN. RLIN has a very small number of cataloging participants compared to OCLC, which has fourteen times as many users as RLIN at present. Among that small group, no more than fifteen RLG institutions were represented at the time of data collection; interestingly enough, those libraries provided us with most of member copies in RLIN. Prior to settling on the current mode of operation, Davis staff had studied the cataloging practices of all RLG member libraries and had been satisfied by the quality of their records. Having determined the acceptability of RLG copies, we now treat them as we do the Library of Congress records. As a consequence, our distributor has only to ascertain the cataloging agency symbol to know what level of cataloger should be assigned to handle the copy.

Both systems have a method of indicating the level of cataloging, but

our study indicated that OCLC's "Level I" designation, or standard cataloging, is not a consistent or reliable indicator of quality. On the other
hand, we have found that RLIN's "Standard" or "non-Standard" cataloging indicator is dependable to a large measure. With "Standard" designation, we would assume full coding, adequate subject analysis and
name and subject headings to have been verified in current authoritative
sources. On the other hand, the presence of "non-Standard" designation
alerts the cataloging staff to the possibility of deficiency or error in the
record. Thus, while not a foolproof system, RLIN's system of designating
the cataloging levels helps catalogers to be alert to possible problems.
Although RLIN's quality control mechanism rests on an honor system, it
works surprisingly well. Its success thus far, we believe, is due largely to
the small size of its community, which enables self-policing to work satis-
factorily. It is also undeniable that the resolve on the part of RLG members to abide by the rules for the common purpose is a strong element for
its success.

The second area of concern is the increased responsibility for copy-
catalogers. Because of their consistency and high reliability, most RLG
member copies are treated in the same way as LC records. The run-of-
the-mill copy-cataloging is, therefore, quite routinized. Given OCLC
member copies, however, copy-catalogers would be required to pay more
attention to coding and to supply additional data where necessary, to
ascertain that MARC tags and contents match, and to supply notes when
our practice requires them. The introduction of complexity and variability
to an existing routine will be hardly ignored by persons affected, and
inevitably a question will be asked: "Should we raise the level of copy-
cataloging staff, who process OCLC member copies?" The lack of appropriate subject headings and insufficient specificity of subject headings
which appeared in some of the sample records from OCLC are problems
which cannot be solved at this level of employees and present still more
complex problems.

The third area of concern would be the effect on the workload of the
professional cataloging staff. The Gray study did not attempt to discuss
whether OCLC cataloging would increase or decrease the professional
workload, but in the case of Health Sciences Library, the professional
cataloger was assigned additional duties after converting to OCLC. While
we do not believe the same process would necessarily occur in the Main
Library, it is a possibility. At a minimum, it appears that some extra
professional time would be mandated to provide decisions relative to the
treatment of member contributed records, because there is currently no
convenient method to assess their quality. It is also probable that a larger
number of member catalog records would require professional staff attention.

One of the eloquent points made by OCLC in support of its shared cataloging was that once a book is cataloged, no second cataloger need be involved in processing it. If the library followed that philosophy and decided to adopt OCLC with no increase, or minimal increase, in professional participation in processing member copies, the Gray paper indicates that a relaxation of the local cataloging standards would follow. While the examination of member copies from OCLC revealed that the reputation for poor quality of the OCLC member copy has been exaggerated, our analyses of the samples from OCLC and RLIN resulted in a judgment that generally less meticulously constructed records were obtained from OCLC, and some of the deficiencies could lead to possible long-term weaknesses in the catalog. To illustrate, if the decision to use minimal professional participation in handling copy were to be implemented, one of the known outcomes would be a certain reduction of catalog records with appropriately specific subject headings. This prospect will naturally lead to questions such as, "How will this deficiency impair patron access to the material, now and in the future?" and "Is the library prepared to sustain willingly a degree of impairment caused by the lack of specificity in subject headings?" They are extremely complex and difficult problems, for which we have no ready answer. Nonetheless, Davis would not opt to join OCLC at this time, knowing that such a move, without increased scrutiny of member copy quality, would mean a lowering of our cataloging standards.

As indicated earlier, the original plan for the Gray study included a section on the catalog maintenance functions in the two systems, but unfortunately, that portion of the study has yet to be performed. Without results from the catalog maintenance study, our preference for RLIN must be stated in a somewhat tentative manner. The experience of investigation and analysis to date has reinforced our belief that the most important elements in the decision to select a bibliographic utility are the individual library's requirements and their priorities. In a situation where contending candidates are as well-matched as OCLC and RLIN, the role of the library's requirements becomes even more critical in the final decision making.

As a final remark, we wish to address one aspect of the quality of the OCLC member copy. During the study we found many fine catalog records contributed by OCLC member libraries that were equal in quality to the best of RLG member copies; thus we know that OCLC includes superb cataloging agencies in its membership. Unfortunately, however, their skills are not fully utilized because of the system's design for display of the database record: that is, if it is not the first catalog to reach the database, even an excellent record cannot be retained in the database to be seen and used by other libraries. The ENHANCE capability, which has been in discussion for some time between OCLC and some of its users would improve the quality of the member copy by allowing designated libraries to upgrade database records. The presence of improved records would also make unnecessary repeated upgrading of the same records by libraries which register a hit but find the record inadequate. Thus we regard the ENHANCE capability to be an important improvement for OCLC and its members and hope for an early implementation.

FACULTY STATUS AND PARTICIPATIVE GOVERNANCE IN ACADEMIC LIBRARIES

Donald D. Hendricks

INTRODUCTION

Of all the perennial concerns of academic librarians, faculty status continues high among the leaders. Reports of regional and national surveys among academic librarians reveal the strong probability that 75% of academic librarians have faculty status, but more specific surveys conducted in some states show a very uneven application of faculty benefits to librarians. These more recent surveys show that conditions today are not very different from those revealed by the Veit and Hintz surveys dating back to 1960 and 1968. There is a divergence of some large proportions in actual practice concerning faculty status among academic institutions.

The question of what happens when academic librarians achieve faculty status on their campus comes down to something like this, "They have it,

Advances in Library Administration and Organization, volume 1, pages 127–137 now what do they do with it?'' It appears that the first arrangement made provides for the conducting of business in the same way an academic teaching department conducts its affairs. Collegiality introduced into an essentially hierarchical environment causes some serious problems. Does the answer for libraries lie in participative management? If it does, the art of administration must come into play to make participative management worthwhile. Here are some ways for establishing participative management and achieving a significant level of collegial governance.

Peer Selection

The choice of colleagues is always a faculty prerogative, but full democratization of the employment process in libraries is often impeded by administrative resistance. The process is complicated today by the Fair Employment Practices procedures. Praise given to a library director because of the staff "he or she built" will not be heard as frequently. Whether a staff is better selected through the group process than "hand picked" by a library director is difficult to assess. In the latter case, direct responsibility for recruiting successes or failures can be ascribed. In the group process, even though the library director has final responsibility, the politics of committee interaction and group dynamics can all cloud the employment action. It is assumed that all librarians accept responsibility for the quality of the library faculty and that in order to fulfill that responsibility, they will organize themselves in such a way as to advance the quality of the faculty through higher recruiting standards and by promoting professional growth for present members.

Personnel Committee

A typical personnel recruiting policy usually provides for a review group, often a committee. A typical Personnel Committee consists of three members: two elected by the staff for staggered terms and one appointed by the director. The committee will review and screen all applicants for positions of library assistants (unclassified support staff) and professional librarians. For our purposes, we will discuss only professional recruiting.

In the review and interview process for professional librarians, the personnel committee is joined by the head of the unit in which the vacancy exists. After the interview and review process, insuring that all equal employment compliances have been met, the committee makes its recommendation to the director of the library. The director may choose to employ the committee preferred candidate or select another lower on the list, or may reject all recommendations.

Tenure and Promotion

Once a library faculty decides it wants to play the "faculty" game, it then must decide on the rules. Unfortunately, too often the game is entered before the participants fully understand the contest. Are the players willing to play "according to Hoyle," that is, by the same standards that control tenure and promotion for other faculty, or do they want to play the game by some modified rules that suit their particular team? The rules are frequently modified by the rationale of the basic service commitment required by the librarian, which leaves little time for traditional research. The service commitment, defined as a teaching role, thus becomes the rationale for changing the game plan. If the other teams in other departments will accept this rationale, then the library team has won an initial victory—they have access to the rewards of tenure, sabbaticals, research funds, and so forth.

Although the other teams may overtly accept the librarian team into the campus game, frequently the feeling that there is a basic difference lingers, and, even worse, the library players have done little to dispel this feeling. For details of a recommended "game" plan, the reader should refer to the ACRL model criteria listed first in the bibliography.

Staff Development

An effective academic library has a valuable resource in its professional staff and the continued growth and development of this resource is essential. Staff development strengthens the capability of an organization to perform its mission more effectively by encouraging and providing for the growth of its human resources. Staff development affirms the ability of the individual and the organization to grow and of each to contribute to the other. Staff development makes the most of the present potential and prepares the individual and the organization for the future.

Effective staff development programs include in-service training for improved operations, short courses, workshops and conferences. Some activities are developed in-house or on campus to meet the expressed needs of the staff, and advantage can be taken of appropriate offerings by library schools or professional groups. This segment of professional concern naturally lends itself to staff initiative and implementation. The administration need only encourage such interest.

Research Committee

Another effective means of promoting staff development and keeping the concepts of research and publication before the library faculty is through the efforts of a research committee. This group seeks to identify and promote research opportunities, and encourages library faculty members to develop areas of study and seek funding.

The committee serves as an advisory body to the library director, pointing out areas in which research endeavor would be helpful. They recommend policy and priority to determine which requests for leave or sabbaticals should be supported. If research funds are available from the university, the committee keeps library faculty informed of this fact, the time cycle involved, and the likelihood of funding for certain projects. They also act as an internal review board, recommending which projects should be endorsed for university funding. This prereview process strengthens the library case in receiving university funding.

Obviously, a research committee can be of great help in the identification of sources for research or study funding, and in assisting library faculty members in proposal preparation, requesting release time, and so forth. By keeping the research climate before the faculty, one can anticipate greater awareness of the need, purpose and opportunity for them to become involved.

Travel

It is an exceptional situation that allows an adequate amount of travel funds for professional purposes. A guideline of 1% of the budget for travel and staff development seems defensible. In a library with a million-dollar budget, not a lot in these times, a library would then ask for $10,000 in travel. Probably this will exceed the amount available in some academic departments and the request would be very vulnerable. Some parameters must be introduced to equalize travel opportunities. Here, a travel committee can be very useful.

Such a committee, partially elected and/or partially appointed, can establish guidelines for the allocation of travel funds. It might decide that presentation of a paper warrants full reimbursement for attendance, while service on a professional committee deserves somewhat less. Simply attending a conference may only count toward remission of either the travel cost or the per diem incurred, or perhaps some fraction such as one-half the total expense. It is not unusual for every staff member to be allocated a sum (unfortunately, usually only a few hundred dollars a year) to spend as he or she sees fit. And it is not at all rare for librarians to attend conferences entirely at their own expense.

When funds are available, committee policy insures that the staff newcomer has a chance to get started in professional activities by some support of expenses. Some portion of the budget is set aside for required attendance at meetings by administrators or representatives.

In addition to providing a forum for development of policy, a travel committee can review proposed travel plans and recommend a certain level of funding. A form can be devised, and often is, indicating the unit supervisor's sanction (as stations must be manned) and perhaps the library director's approval. The form specifies the purpose of the travel and the anticipated expenses. The committee reviews the purpose and the amount and suggests a level of support. The traveler might choose to appeal the recommendation or decide not to go; the director can adjust the recommendation downward or upward, depending on staff priorities; and at least the staff has a representative group involved in the decisions that affect their mutual perquisites.

THE SERVICE ARENA

Bibliographic Instruction

The recent flurry of developments in bibliographic instruction is an opportunity for great enhancement of the role of the librarian as a faculty member. The contact may vary from a classroom visit or orientation tour to a formal semester course of instruction, but the librarians' participation strengthens the role of librarian as an equal partner in the educational process. Guiding the student through the intricacies of library access is no meager task, if done well. Furthermore, as automation makes a greater impact on information retrieval and analysis, as card catalogs close and microtext and terminal access replace the card catalog, this phase of classroom interaction becomes more important. Sessions in research courses and graduate seminars are of particular value in that they review the specialized resources helpful in independent study.

Even in a medium-sized academic library there is a need for a coordinator of these teaching activities. Faculty recognition of the "teaching" portion of the librarians' "service" obligation can be facilitated through this medium. Sometimes, this librarian is called a Bibliographic Instruction Coordinator, or the Instructional Services Librarian, a somewhat more preferable title.

Instructional Services Librarian

This person has the responsibility for organizing, coordinating and carrying out a wide variety of public relations and interpretative tasks. The best use of the library and its various services are enhanced by using all opportunities to enlarge upon and communicate about these endeavors. Specific responsibilities in this position might be:

1. Bibliographic instruction: Supervise a major program of bibliographic instruction which provides service to nearly 10,000 students annually. This involves direct responsibility for freshman

instructional program, the provision of advanced instruction upon request, and the coordination of bibliographic instruction throughout the library system.

2. "Information Services in Today's Society" (Books & Libraries): Develop and plan this program, achieve its implementation in the curriculum as a one hour elective course, organize and teach sections as needed. Coordinate staffing of other sections, when necessary.

3. Tours: Devise standard tours for the various age groups requesting tours. Arrange guides, scheduling, and so forth.

4. Slide lectures: Schedule and staff all general library lectures. Create standardized lectures for (1) high school students, and (2) college freshmen. Prepare list of review questions to accompany lectures. Coordinate special lectures (Govt. Doc., ERIC. etc.) Schedule and staff off-campus lectures as requested.

5. Library publications: Revise as needed, content of library manuals to make them complement the other library instruction programs. Instructional Services would also be responsible for internal and external newsletters and informational materials.

6. Public relations: Cultivate and maintain contacts with faculty and community to encourage positive use of Bibliographic Instruction facilities. Coordinate the program with that of others in the community, (i.e., be familiar with public library programs). Seek and implement opportunities for staff development.

7. Statistics: Keep statistics on tours, lectures, and so forth, for annual report and/or possible revision of program.

8. Other special projects as assigned.

The Reference or Subject Bibliographer

Many academic libraries abandoned the divisional plan of organization because of staff expense and space restriction; though in any effort to acquire and maintain faculty recognition, the divisional structure would seem the most appropriate—and supportive.

A setting that combines a special desk and staff, surrounded by the indexing tools and reference guides germane to the disciplines represented and adjacent to the current periodicals and regular stack material provides a unique base from which to work. Without concern for reserve books, circulation functions, or cataloging processes, the reference bibliographer working from such an environment is able to implement almost the ideal situation for aiding a patron. The intellectual process of guiding the inquirer to the best sources is aided in such a case. Consulting with a faculty member about a research problem or recommending new acquisitions flows naturally from this environment. Compared with an assigned two-hour session at a general reference desk, where the tools of the trade and related materials are far-flung, this arrangement seems conducive to a more satisfactory professional life, and helpful in achieving a partnership level in the eyes of the faculty. A departmental setting could achieve the same thing, but often such departments are very small and lack adequate supporting staff.

Without adequate support staff a librarian gets bogged down in operational aspects which are essential but diminish the opportunities to interact effectively with graduate students and faculty. In addition, even with the best guidelines or subject definition, the scattering of materials in a departmental plan will inhibit, at least the appearance, if not the fact of subject control and effective library management.

BUDGET PREPARATION

Financial planning is probably the most difficult area to orchestrate, yet if done successfully, is most conducive to welding staff goals. Staff input is extremely valuable. Whether the institution is in a growth period, a stable situation, or, more common today, a period of decline, staff awareness of these considerations forces a realistic view of the fiscal environment.

A fiscal planning committee charged with developing design of a three-year or five-year plan for coping with either the expansion or constriction of finances, can be very effective. Data predicting the direction and scale of student enrollment can be used; past inflation rates of library materials provide another element of design; curricula changes that seem to indicate long-term effects should be carefully considered. The reallocation of resources based on a two- or four-semester trend is unwise and expensive, but the committee can be alert to subtle or obvious shifts and changes which augur long-term effects for the curricular pattern of the institution. Based on the long-range plan, individual years can be worked out easily. This statement may serve as a model charge.

The Budget Committee shall consist of five members. The University Senate's library representative shall serve *ex officio* as chairman. The other four members shall be one appointee and one electee each from technical service and public service. The appointees are chosen by the library director. The terms of office shall be two years.

The charge to the committee, which serves mainly to assist the director, shall include: (1) to advise the director; (2) to prepare reports; (3) to conduct reviews of budget requests; and (4) to see that each stage of budget action is conducted as scheduled.

The areas to be reviewed by the committee will include equipment, supplies, travel and new positions, whether classified, technical, paraprofessional or professional.

The annual budget cycle shall include the following:

1. The director or the committee chairman will give all persons concerned at least a one-month notice to prepare their budget requests for the subsequent fiscal year.
2. Each respondent will present the request in writing to the Budget Committee by the date designated. The list may be annotated to justify or clarify need.
3. After preliminary review by the director and the committee, copies of all requests will be made available for library faculty inspection at least three days prior to a discussion meeting.

The Budget Committee will hold an open discussion of budget requests. Two purposes are envisioned here: an opportunity for a requestor to explain why a particular item is needed, and a chance for the director and the committee to derive a sense of priorities and urgency for various needs.

On the basis of information derived, the committee in session will prepare a final draft of the budget for presentation to university officials. This final document will be available for library faculty inspection prior to presentation. When the director receives official notice of the approved budget, he/she will make a formal presentation to the library faculty.

The process described here, coupled with the long-range elements discussed earlier, should accomplish several things. It gives staff a concept of institutional direction and goals, and how the library unit fits therein. It gives the staff the sense of participation in long-range planning as well as a strong actual role in the yearly fiscal management. The budget process described could provide the library faculty a strong voice in budget design. A united common effort, based on understanding and participation, should result as a consequence of this process.

PUBLICATIONS

Publications representing the various service features of an academic library are an excellent avenue for the novice, or anyone who has written very little, to explore the opportunities available. Librarians are accused of being generalists, without the type of in-depth knowledge necessary for publication. To get started in writing, academic librarians can also look at their own area, in bibliography, to synthesize and interrelate a variety of fields. Bibliographic work reveals the content of one library to interested users and is helpful in curriculum support. This approach is useful in correlating the contents of a number of libraries in a local area to establish and demonstrate the strength in holdings of a particular topic. From this, it is a short step to relating other fields to library science and it to other areas. Collection guides or "Pathfinders" are a form of such compilation; these can be developed into comprehensive reviews of subjects to indicate the depth of support for graduate investigation or a particular topic in a local or regional setting. The benefits of computer applications in this kind of work are obvious. Library handbooks or descriptions are also good beginnings in the publication effort; though modest, handbooks are a valid contribution in that they distill much information for library patrons.

A Publication Committee is a useful adjunct to these endeavors; it can insure that quality is maintained, and that there is continuity and cohesion in a publication program. Committee members can stimulate effort on new publications and identify projects for staff. Larger libraries find a Publications Coordinator helpful, and a Publications Committee can serve as an advisory body.

Usually people are eager to describe their jobs and their activities. Used intelligently, library publications can become a focal point for such communications in announcements and newsletters. These efforts are excellent beginnings—future, more in-depth work can then be encouraged and proceed from this environment.

PLANNING

The planning process—setting objectives, identifying alternatives, choosing the best alternative, evaluating the product against the original objective—is an ongoing activity in libraries. Library directors have been doing this, theoretically, right along. Why should it be an organized, even a separate, activity?

The process itself, involving of staff, becomes very important in establishing the faculty self-governance concept. Setting of objectives for each unit and level of the organization is required before rational planning can result. The probable conditions and environment in which these objectives will perform must then be described. What funding level can a library reasonably expect three or five years ahead? Which curricular areas will be developed, which diminished? What are the space requirements? How many staff members are needed? Which activities will be automated? When can these transfers be scheduled? These projections may or may not be within staff control. The identified goals, to operate within the environment defined as well as can be, must be internally consistent, and fit within the goals of the university itself.

An academic library is a complex operation; actions taken in one part of the unit will frequently have an effect on another part. Thus, broad staff participation in the planning process is essential to achievement of reasonable ends. Each supervisor has a special knowledge and perspective.

All related information must be known to avoid false starts or duplicative efforts.

All employees desire to have a say in the events that affect their working situation. If staff members are encouraged to participate in planning, they are, to some degree, responsible for this environment. This raises morale, lessens friction and increases productivity. Needed changes become acceptable when one has a hand in their identification.

Planning and decision making on both economic and political levels requires improvement by librarians. This is an especially fruitful area for the application of faculty governance concepts upon library management.

SUMMARY

Implementation of the degree of participative management described here could lead to several perceived or real problems.

A variety of committees gives many people an opportunity to serve; unfortunately, in libraries as in other academic units, the same people seem to be elected and appointed. People with good ideas may be bypassed because of personality clashes or a reluctance to carry out assignments.

Not all of these committees and activities would function simultaneously or be deemed appropriate in a given setting, but if the committee system is not directed or orchestrated, anarchy can result, with the unit floundering aimlessly. As committees change and personalities differ, the unit goals could fluctuate and confusion would destroy morale and waste time. New energies and ideas are strengths in committee changes, but there is a vulnerable line to be drawn between new approaches and the need both to reach the agreed objectives and to accomplish their continued revision.

There is little new in these remarks, but this essay is an attempt to summarize some of the techniques used in academic departments and in libraries to achieve a true sense of academic governance.

REFERENCES

American Library Association, Association of College and Research Libraries, "Model Statement of Criteria and Procedures for Appointment, Promotion in Academic Rank, and Tenure for College and University Librarians," *College and Research Library News* 34:192–95 (Sept. 1973).

Bailey, Martha J., "Some Effects of Faculty Status on Supervision in Academic Libraries," *College and Research Libraries* 37:48–52 (Jan. 1976).

Byerly, Greg, "The Faculty Status of Academic Librarians in Ohio," *College and Research Libraries* 41:422–29 (Sept. 1980).

Gauryck, Jacquelyn A., "The SUNY Librarians' Faculty Status Game," *Journal of Academic Librarianship*, Vol. 1, No. 3, pp. 11–13 (July 1975).

Hawkins, JoAnne, et. al., "The Status of Status: The Status of Librarians in Texas Academic Libraries," (Austin: University of Texas at Austin Libraries, 1978) ED 178042.

Hintz, Carl, "Criteria for Appointment to and Promotion in Academic Rank," *College and Research Libraries* 29:341–46 (Sept. 1968).

Reid, Marion T., et. al., "The Role of the Academic Librarian in Library Governance," *New Horizons of Academic Libraries* (ACRL, 1978).

Schmidt, C. James, "A Letter to H. W. Axford," *Journal of Academic Librarianship*, Vol. 2, No. 6, pp. 281–82 (Jan. 1977).

Sparks, David G. E., "Academic Librarianship: Professional Strivings and Political Realities," *College and Research Libraries* 41:408–21 (Sept. 1980).

Veit, Fritz, "The Status of the Librarian According to Accrediting Standards of Regional and Professional Associations," *College and Research Libraries* 21:127–35 (Mar. 1960).

BIOGRAPHICAL SKETCH
OF THE CONTRIBUTORS

Dr. Edwin B. Brownrigg is a specialist in the areas of library automation and administration, and computer center management. He has held positions as Head of the Systems Office and Director of Academic Computing at New York University; archivist, bibliographer, and librarian at the New York Public Library; and has taught at Queens College and St. Johns University in New York. He received his MLS from Columbia University and undergraduate and advanced degrees from New York University. Dr. Brownrigg has published extensively in the area of library automation. He is currently Director of the Division of Library Automation at the University of California.

Robert F. Byrnes, Specialist in Russian and East European History, is Distinguished Professor of History at Indiana University. A graduate of Amherst College and Harvard University, Byrnes held a senior fellowship in the Russian Institute of Columbia University 1948–50 and was at the Institute for Advanced Study at Princeton in 1954. He has received three honorary doctoral degrees. Dr. Byrnes has published extensively in the field of European history with particular emphasis upon Russia. He has lectured extensively in colleges and universities in this country and abroad.

Ms. Dailey formerly was Chief Librarian for Technical Services, City College of the City University of New York and is now Assistant University Librarian for Technical Services and Automation at UC Davis. She is a reviewer and panelist for the National Endowment for the Humanities.

Diana Gray of the Catalog Department is the Research Library Information Network Coordinator, and was formerly a staff member of the University of California, San Diego Library.

Donald D. Hendricks received his Master of Arts in Library Science from the University of Michigan in 1955, and his doctorate in Library Science from Illinois in 1966. He has had a variety of experiences in academic and medical libraries, having served as Director of Libraries at Sam Houston State University, Huntsville, Texas, and at the University of Texas Health Science Center in Dallas. Hendricks has authored a number of articles. Since 1978 he has been Director of Libraries at the University of New Orleans.

Ms. Jaroff, Head of the Computer Input Section of the Systems and Automation Department of the Shields Library, supervises data processing for an inhouse serials system. In her spare time she does research on organizational humor.

William C. Roselle is a graduate of Thiel College, and holds his M.L.S. from the University of Pittsburgh. Mr. Roselle has served in a variety of library posts for the State Library of Pennsylvania, Carnegie-Mellon University, Pennsylvania State University, and the University of Iowa. For the past ten years, he has served as professor and director of the library at the University of Wisconsin-Milwaukee.

Allen B. Veaner is University Librarian at the Santa Barbara Campus of the University of California. Veaner did his undergraduate work at Gettysburg College and in 1960 received the M.L.S. from Simmons College which recently designated him as recipient of the 1981 Simmons Alumni Achievement Award. He is the founding editor of Microform Review and has published several books and numerous articles on automation, micrographics and administration. Before coming to the University of California he was employed at Harvard University and Stanford University. He has been active in library education through the ALA's Committee on Accreditation.

AUTHOR INDEX

SUBJECT INDEX

Foundations in
LIBRARY AND INFORMATION SCIENCE

A Series of Monographs, Texts and Treatises

Series Editor: **Robert D. Stueart**
Dean Graduate School of Library and Information Science
Simmons College, Boston

"Librarians and library school faculty members are becoming accustomed to finding the volumes of this series among the most useful studies of their subjects."
—JOURNAL OF ACADEMIC LIBRARIANSHIP

OPTIONS FOR THE 80s

Proceedings of the Second National Conference of the Association of College and Research Libraries, October 1-4, 1981, Minneapolis, Minnesota

Virgil F. Massman
Executive Director,
James J. Hill Reference Library
St. Paul, Minnesota

Edited by

Michael D. Kathman
Director of Libraries, College of St.
Benedict and St. John's University
Collegeville, Minnesota

(Volume 17 in **Foundations in Library and Information Science**
A Series of Monographs, Texts and Treatises - Edited by **Robert D. Stueart**)

In preparation. June 1982, Ca. 800 pp.
ISBN 0-89232-276-4

The Second National Conference of the Association for College and Research Libraries has taken as its focus an assessment of the options that lie before us in the next decade.

This volume will contain 56 papers present on a variety of topics. They will include: Information Services and Bibliographic instruction; Special Collections and Facilities, Performance Evaluation and Governance; Networking, Cooperation and Technology; Standards and Collection Development; Administration and Funding; The Role of the Library and the Librarian in Academic Institutions; and Planning and Bibliographic Control.

In addition, invited papers on major issues as well as the text of the five theme addresses will be presented in an attempt to identify the major opportunities and challenges that confront higher education and academic and research libraries during the 1980s.

JAI PRESS INC., 36 Sherwood Place, P.O. Box 1678
Greenwich, Connecticut 06836
Telephone: 203-661-7602   Cable Address: JAIPUBL

THE LIBRARY QUARTERLY

Recipient of the 1981 ALA/RTSD
Blackwell/North America Scholarship Award as the
outstanding publication of 1980 in the field of
acquisitions, collection development and related areas
of resources development in libraries.

Collection Development in Libraries

A Treatise

Edited by **Robert D. Stueart**
Dean, Graduate School of Library and Information Science, Simmons College-Boston
and **George B. Miller, Jr.**
Assistant Director for Collection Development
University of New Mexico Libraries

(Volume 10 of **Foundations in Library and Information Sciences**
A Series of Monographs, Texts and Treatises.
Series Editor: **Robert D. Stueart**)

"The first major treatise on collection development as it has developed in the United States. . . It
should be acquired by all large libraries."   *— JOURNAL OF ACADEMIC LIBRARIANSHIP*

Part A, 1980, 300 pp.
ISBN 0-89232-106-7   LC 79-93165

**CONTENTS: Preface. Introduction. PART I. OVERVIEW. Collection Development in
the United States,** Robert D. Stueart, School of Library Science, Simmons College. **PART II.
COLLECTION MANAGEMENT. Organizational Models for Collection Development,**
Norman H. Dudley, University of California Libraries-Los Angeles. **The Allocation of Money
Within the Book Budget,** Murrary S. Martin, Pennsylvania State University Libraries. **The
Formulation of a Collection Development Policy Statement,** Shelia T. Dowd, University of
California Libraries-Berkeley. **A Survey of Attitudes Toward Collection Development in
College Libraries,** James C. Baughman, School of Library Science, Simmons College, Andrea
Hoffman, Teacher's College Library, Columbia University, Linda Rambler, Pennsylvania State
University Libraries, Donald Ungarelli, Long Island University Libraries and Harvey Varnet, Bristol
Community College Learning Resources Center. **Resource Sharing in Collection
Development,** John R. Kaiser, Pennsylvania State University Libraries. **Managing Library
Collection: The Process of Review and Pruning,** Paul H. Mosher, Stanford University
Libraries. **PART III. COLLECTION DEVELOPMENT PROCESS. The Selection Process,**
Jean Boyer Hamlin, Rutgers University Libraries-Newark. **Mass Buying Programs in the
Development Process,** Robert D. Stueart, School of Library Science, Simmons College.
Collecting Foreign Materials from Latin America, Carl W. Deal, University of Illinois
Libraries. **Collecting Foreign Materials from Western Europe,** Erwin Welsch, University of
Minnesota Libraries. **The Role of Retrospective Materials in Collection Development,** A.
Dean Larsen, Brigham Young University Libraries. **"Collection Officer" or "Collector": The
Preservation Side of the "Development" Responsibility,** Pamela W. Darling, Columbia
University Libraries.

Part B, 1980, 300 pp.
ISBN 0-89232-162-8   LC 79-93165

JAI PRESS INC., 36 Sherwood Place, P.O. Box 1678
Greenwich, Connecticut 06836
Telephone: 203-661-7602   Cable Address: JAIPUBL